Kālaśakti

Bhartṛhari's Philosophy of Time

Dedication

जगन्नाथः स्वामी नयनपथगामी भवतु मे

Jagannāthaḥ svāmī nayanapathagāmī bhavatu me

I decicate everything,
O Lord of the universe!
– my body, my soul,
my *dharma*, my *karma*,
my good deeds, my follies –
at your Lotus Feet.

Preface

WHILE working on the manuscript of a book *Śabda: A Study of Bhartṛhari's Philosophy of Language,* I felt quite uncomfortable with the idea of *kāla* (Time). My problem was how to accommodate this concept within the scope of philosophy of language. My training in Western philosophy of language created a sort of mental block, for all along I had entertained a dogma that "time" as a concept properly belongs to the area of metaphysics and it has nothing to do with our understanding of how language as principle functions. But sooner I realized that the Indian philosophical tradition looks at "language" from a different perspective than the Western way of viewing it.

Our tradition focuses primarily on language as "speech". So we pay attention to certain issues that is yet to draw the attention of the Western thinkers. Our philosophers hotly debate about how the hearer grasps the "sense" as the speaker utters the words in a sequence. The peculiar nature of our speech is that it cannot be uttered as whole. By the time we utter the first syllable it is lost and is replaced by the next syllable, and the process goes on till the whole utterance is completed. This automatically leads us to the notion of sequence and then to time. Gradually I realized that Bhartṛhari's analysis of language remains incomplete without his metaphysics, that again is woven around the principle of "language". This also helped me to uproot another deep-seated bias that academic philosophers need not tread into the area of metaphysics. I realized that there is nothing to feel apologetic about going deep into the metaphysical issues.

I chose the theme *Kālaśakti* as I hoped to examine the concept both from metaphysical as well as semantic dimensions. But the choice of the topic posed a huge challenge for me. There was enormous paucity of literature on this area of study in English. As such the concept of time in Indian philosophy has not got the attention of the scholars that it deserves. But in the case of Bhartṛhari, the state of affairs is still disturbing. There is virtually no book on *Kālaśakti*. The only works that could be of some help were the translation of *Kālasamuddeśa* by P.S. Sharma and the translation of K.A.S. Iyer along with the other *Samuddeśa*'s of the Prakīrṇa-kāṇḍa of *Vākyapadīya*. Even the Bengali book *Bhartṛharir Darsane Kalerdhara* by P.K. Majumdar is also a Bengali translation of *Kālasamuddeśa* with Helārāja's commentary. There are also very few papers published on the concept of *Kālaśakti* of Bhartṛhari. So my task was really challenging. At the same time I found it worthwhile to undertake it.

Initially, the project was undertaken as the UGC Emeritus Fellow. But I needed more time to go into the depth of the topic. My sickness for the last five months had given me enough scope to go through the work as I was spared of all the household responsibilities. I am grateful to my son Prof. Priyadarshi Patnaik for his suggestion that this could be the right opportunity for me to keep me happy. My daughter-in-law Arundhati, my husband Madan Mohan Patnaik and my granddaughter Pihu saw to it that I finish my task without any hassles. I am grateful to them. My sincerest gratitude to Susheel Mittal of D.K. Printworld who stood by me in my travails of life; and his willingness to publish the manuscript.

18 June 2014 **Tandra Patnaik**

Cataloging in Publication Data — DK
[Courtesy: D.K. Agencies (P) Ltd. <docinfo@dkagencies.com>]

Patnaik, Tandra.
Kālaśakti : Bhartṛhari's philosophy of time / Tandra Patnaik.
p. cm.
Includes bibliographical references (p.) and index.
ISBN 13: 9788124607589

1. Time. 2. Semantics (Philosophy) 3. Sanskrit language – Grammar. 4. Bhartṛhari. Vākyapadīya. I. Title.

DDC 115 23

ISBN 13: 978-81-246-0758-9
First published in India, in 2014

Printed and published by:
D.K. Printworld (P) Ltd.
Regd. Office : *Vedasri*, F-395, Sudarshan Park
(Metro Station: Ramesh Nagar)
New Delhi – 110 015
Phones : (011) 2545 3975, 2546 6019; *Fax* : 2546 5926
e-mail : indology@dkprintworld.com
Web : www.dkprintworld.com

Kālaśakti

Bhartṛhari's Philosophy of Time

Tandra Patnaik

DK PRINTWORLD
Publishers of Indian Traditions

Contents

1

Introduction

TIME as a concept permeates our life. We talk of time both in generic sense like "only time will tell", "time and tide waits for none", etc. as well as in particularized sense like "what is the time now?", "how much time it will take to travel from Delhi to Mumbai?". Despite such recurrent use in the wide spheres of activity based on the notion of time, the question – What is Time? – may seem to be the most perplexing one even for the most systematic thinker, not only Indian but any thinking human person in general. The concept is too common yet equally too subtle for a definite human thought and expression. Here I would like to quote St Augustine who very aptly voices the bewilderment of a man faced with the question – What is Time?

> Who can readily and briefly explain this? Who can even in thought comprehend it so as to utter a word about it? But what in discourse do we mention more familiarly and knowingly than Time? And we understand when we speak of it; we understand also when we hear it spoken by another. What then is Time? If no one asks me, I know; if I wish to explain it to one that asketh, I know not.[1]

In Indian tradition the word time that is mostly referred to as *kāla*[2] is much more complex. Every aspect of an Indian life

---

[1] St Augustine, *Confessions*, Book XI.17.

[2] *Kāla* and many compound words using *kāla* are very common in many Indian languages – *kālacakra, akāla, nityakāla, dīrghakāla, śarbakāle, kālekāle,* etc.

including birth and death, marriage and matchmaking, journey and beginning of any activity is determined by *kāla* – auspicious time (*śubha kāla*) and (*aśubha kāla*). A number of other words like *samaya, ṛtu, velā, kṣaṇa* and *muhūrta* are also used to refer to this aspect of time. The concept of *kāla* has played a key role in Indian culture – literature, astronomy, social and religious life as well as in philosophy. In India there existed different Śāstras (sciences) that dealt with the phenomenal time, such as Vyākaraṇa (grammar), Jyotiṣa (astronomy and astrology), Dharma and Nīti (precepts), Vāstu (architecture), Saṅgīta (music), Citra (painting), Sthāpatya (sculpture), Āyurveda (medicine), etc. Interestingly, in our tradition the word *kāla* is again used to epitomize the Time personified, like Time as death, Time as the supreme reality, Time as a cycle, Time as destiny and so forth. In the Indian context the problem is doubly perplexing when the philosophers and thinkers try to relate time (the measurable, durable/non-durable phenomenon of the phenomenal world) with the Time that is beyond measurement, beyond division and beyond calculable duration. The problem specifically haunts varied metaphysical and religious systems that come forward to handle this baffling issue with equal disparity depending on their favoured metaphysical stance.

Kāla in Ancient Tradition: Diverse Spectrum

The etymological root of the term *kāla* is √*kal*, which means to count (cf. Latin *calculo*).[3] Thus according to some, the word *kāla* signifies that which can count up the age of all. Time is also that which is used as the basis of measuring temporal units such as moments, seconds, minutes, hours, days, years and even eons. Again, *kāla* also means "that devours every being". The root √*kal* also signifies "to devour", which leads to the ascription of the destructive power to Time. Thus, *kāla*

[3] Monier-Williams, *Sanskrit-English Dictionary*, p. 104.

also refers to death. The different nuances of the word *kāla* can be seen in *Bhagavad-Gītā* in the various utterances of Lord Kṛṣṇa.

kālaḥ kalayatāmaham ।

Of calculators I am Time.
– X.30

kālo 'smi, lokakṣayakṛt . . . . ।

Time am I world-destroying.
– XI.32

Here the supreme spirit as the destroyer of the universe is seen as a personification of the destructive principle, which is identified with Time. Again, in the same treatise *kāla* has been also identified with the God, the Supreme Principle.

aham evākṣayaḥ kālo . . . ।

I also am imperishable Time.[4]
– X.33

The grammarian–philosopher Bhartṛhari offers another interesting analysis of the etymology of the term. He uses the word *kāla* in the sense of *kālayati* (turning out) to mean the activities and dynamism of the all-pervasive Time that drives the objects (*kālaḥ* = objects) of the world[5] (3.9.14). Besides in certain works of non-philosophical genre the term *kāla* is used to stand for destiny. However, broadly speaking, the etymological significance of the word refers to two dimensions of the concept: the phenomenal time that is relative and has parts; and the all-pervasive principle that is beyond division and calculation.[6]

---

4 The translation of quotations from *Bhagavad-Gītā* are from S. Radhakrishan, 1977.

5 *Vākyapadīya* III.9.14 (henceforth *Vākyapadīya* shall be referred to as *VP*).

6 I shall be using *Kāla* with capital K and Time with capital T while referring to the notion in the absolute sense as a principle.

A look at the Indian cultural tradition reveals that *kāla* as a concept has a very ancient origin. It has played an important role both in the works of Vedic and non-Vedic origin. But some scholars are of the opinion that the idea of *Kāla* in the generic sense (as an all-pervading principle) was more predominant in heretic and non-Brāhmanic literature. But the connotation of the word *kāla* is not always fixed and it kept on changing in different phases of the development of the Indian intellectual tradition. A brief scanning of the development of the concept may offer us a better idea of how diversely the word has been used.

Interestingly, *Ṛgveda,* the first compendium of the Vedic civilization, does not use the word *kāla* in the sense it is usually used. While *Kāla* is the generic expression for Time, it occurs only once in *Ṛgveda,* and that too in a later section. To the early Vedic agriculturalists and herdsmen, time (*ṛtu*) meant a settled point of time, time appointed for any action (especially sacrifices or worship) and a division of year (seasons).[7] *Ṛgveda* uses the term *kāla* like *ṛtu* not to mean Time but "certain moment" or "right moment" or more appropriately "right moment for a purpose". In *Atharvaveda* and the Brāhmaṇas, the term *ṛtu* was gradually superseded by the word *kāla.* In fact, the first three Vedas – *Ṛg, Sāma* and *Yajur* – talked of Time as an important aspect of human life but seldom noticed it as an abstract concept. It is rather the measurable time that was seen to be closely connected with the sacrifice and rituals (*karma*):

> This time . . . has no reality, that is to say efficiency, except the moments, in which the divine and the sacred acts are concerted.[8]

Thus in these texts Time is seen to be associated with *krama.* But from the available records it has been claimed that there existed a tradition that considered Time as the cosmic power.

---

[7] Monier-Williams, *Sanskrit-English Dictionary.*

[8] Quoted from Panikkar 1976: 64.

Some of them did not exactly belong to the Vedic and Brāhmanic traditions. These traditions are also very ancient and have few analogies in any other civilization. The way the later Brāhmanical tradition vigorously refuted this theory of Time (often called as Kālavāda) makes us infer that the idea once upon a time was quite predominant. However, *Atharvaveda* is the first treatise of the Vedic genre that unambiguously exalts Time as a cosmic and eternal principle. In fact, a series of hymns are dedicated to Time or *Kāla* called Kāla-Sūkta.[9] I quote some such important hymns from the treatise that may help us understand its other nuances:

Time draws (the chariot like) a horse with seven reins,
A thousand-eyed, fruitful-loined, immune to age.
Astride it are poets who understand inspired songs.
Its wheels are everything that exists.

Thus time draws seven wheels,
It has seven hubs, its axle is (called) non-death.
On the hither side of all these existences,
It advances first among the gods.

A full vessel has been placed above Time,
We see (Time) even if it is in many places (at once)
Opposite all these existences
Time (is also seated) they say, in the high firmament.

In oneness Time bore all these existences,
In oneness it encompassed them around.
Time the father became time their son.
No glory higher than his.

Time engendered Heavens above,
Time also (engendered) the earths we see.
Set in motion by Time, things which were
And shall be are assigned their place.

---

9 *Atharvaveda* XXI 53.1-8, quoted from Panikkar, pp. 65-66.

Time created the Earth;
In Time burns the sun;
In time (yes). Time, the eyes see far off
all existences.

In Time is consciousness; in Time breath;
In Time is concentrated the name.
As Time unfolds
all creatures rejoice in it.

In Time is (sacred) Fervour, in Time (yes) in Time
Is concentrated all-powerful Brahman
Time is the lord of all things,
Time was the father of Prajāpati.

These hymns very explicitly posit Time as the first principle that engenders not only the phenomenal world but also the particularized times that is encountered in human experience. The *sūkta* uses very powerful and rich words to enunciate the relation between the cosmic and eternal time (Time) and the empirical time, i.e. the creator and the created; the father and the son, cause and effect. *Kāla* as the all powerful principle is delineated not only to support the space, but also the temporalities that infuse order and harmony to our empirical world. Even the inner realities like consciousness and breath are said to be under the sway of Time. It is the principle of dynamism that sets everything in motion. *Kāla* is conceived here as the supreme divinity that is subjected to neither to the personified creator nor to the impersonal universal powers of the sacrifice or of *Brahman*. So it is claimed:

> After conquering all worlds by the Word, time advances, the supreme god.[10]

Kāla-Sūkta of *Atharvaveda* is of special interest because it uses the term *Brahman* in the context of *Kāla*. From this it may be

[10] Panikkar 1976: 66.

assumed that when this particular Saṁhitā was composed the idea of *Brahman* as the Supreme Reality must have been developed. At the same time it also may be noticed that *Atharvaveda* to some extent contained the ideas that were taken to be non-Brāhmanic in tone and tenor.

The idea of Time as an indomitable and all-pervading force that we notice in *Atharvaveda* was not entirely new to the ancient Indian tradition. The concept of *Kāla* was also used by certain heretic and non-Vedic systems of thought. This becomes evident from two specific *śloka*s in *Śvetāśvatara Upaniṣad* (*ŚvetUp.*) (I.2 and VI.1). These two *śloka*s refute the theory of *Kāla* as the all-pervading powerful principle quite vehemently. The Upaniṣad despises in uncertain terms that such a view is only upheld by the materialist and naturalist. Rejecting their viewpoint the Upaniṣad says:

> Some sages say that the cause of the world is nature, some say it is Time. They are mistaken, it is the power of God which causes the *Brahman*'s wheel to turn in this world. He, then, who is partless, the constant among inconstant, the One of the many, all-maker, all-knower, immortal omnipresent is the creator of time (*kālaḥkāla, kālakāraḥ*).
>
> – *ŚvetUp*. VI.13

We gather from the Buddhist and Jaina literature that there existed certain schools of unorthodox tradition like the Ājīvakas who offered predominant place to *Kāla* as a concept because in their scheme of thought human life lacks freedom of will; and is strictly predetermined by Time. These thinkers not only characterized *Kāla* as all-pervasive force but also considered man a total prisoner of the sovereign called *Kāla*. Here *Kāla* also stands for irreversible human fate. So the protagonists of this viewpoint are called Kālavādins, Niyativādins, Yaddr̥cchavādins. Perhaps the earliest protagonist of the doctrine was Makkhali Goṣāla, the founder of the non-Vedic sect, Ājīvakas. Though during the Upaniṣadic phase the idea of *Kāla* as the indomitable fate was refuted this view seems to be resurrected in a much later works like *Mahābhārata* and certain other Purāṇas. Of course, in *Mahābhārata* one comes across various other dimensions of time but *Kāla,* as an insurmountable fate, gains predominance.

The post-Saṁhitā period (Upaniṣadic phase) reflected a radical departure in the mapping of *kāla* as a concept. The Upaniṣadic literature leaned towards a clear-cut non-dualism. The idea is vaguely presented in the hymn of *Atharvaveda* wherein *Kāla* is said to flow from the vessel of the ultimate dynamic Reality (*Brahman*) which in its unchanging form is timeless, and in the manifested form is the cause of the phenomena. The phenomenal world that is characterized by change and movement of the celestial bodies like sun needs the idea of time to account for the experience as well as the transience of the world of experience. But when we are talking of the ultimate Reality in its unmanifested state there is no change and no movement, hence no need to assume a principle called *Kāla*. So in the ultimate sense *Kāla* is conceived as unreal. In other words, in the principal Upaniṣadic literature *kāla*/ time is projected as a concept that has some relevance only with regard to the phenomenal world; and since the phenomenal world has no independent reality, time too is not an independent reality. The concept of the absolute Time that was eulogized in some of the hymns of *Atharvaveda* is now divested of its ontological significance. A new form of bifurcation is now introduced, viz. between the time-less *Brahman* (as the Absolute Reality transcends Time and temporality) and the empirical/relative time.

But the later Upaniṣads like *Maitrī Upaniṣad* seems to adopt a compromising stand, i.e. between *Brahman* and *kāla*. This Upaniṣad talks of the two forms (*dve rūpe*) of the *Brahman*, i.e. two aspects (*dvaitī bhāva*) of the single essence (*tadekam*) as

Time and the Timeless (*kālas cakālas ca*). "From one who worships", thinking, "Time as *Brahman*" (*kālam brahmeti*), time (*kāla*, also is death) reflows afar. As it has been said:

From Time flows forth all beings,
From Time advance to their full growth,
And in Time again, win home,
Time is the formed (mūrti) *and formless, both.*[11]

There are indeed two forms of *Brahman*; Time and the Timeless. That which is prior to the sun is Timeless (*akāla*) and partless (*akala*) but that which begins with the sun is the time that has parts (*sakala*) from which that of the year, etc. are measured and counted. Here the sun is taken as the basis of the measurement of the time in the phenomenal world. This is why *Muṇḍaka Upaniṣad* says:

> The extended (*vigraha*, specific or hypostatized) time is the regal river of begotten beings . . . (the ultimate source) of All This here and, of whatever fair or foul there is to be seen in this world. – VI.14-16

> Other than "has been" and "shall be", without beginning or end, Lord of what has been shall be, He alone is the today and tomorrow. – *KUp.* III.14

However, by the time theism gained some ground in the Upaniṣadic literature and Purāṇas, the idea of time as a creative force reappeared in a new way, i.e. as the power (*śakti*) of God. *ŚvetUp.* which is one of the first Upaniṣads with a clear theistic flavour declares that:

> It is the Lord who is the knower and creator of Time.[12]

Here Time is seen as the instrument of the Lord. Both in the Vaiṣṇava and Śaiva Purāṇas we notice that *Kāla* is seen as the

---

11 Quoted in Coomaraswamy 1992: 140.

12 *ŚvetUp.* VI.1 and VI.2.

śakti of the deity. *Kālaśakti* is regarded as the instrument of creation, preservation and destruction of the universe. For instance, *Śiva Purāṇa* admits three levels of *kāla*. In the first stage *kāla* is not different from Śiva. It is eternal. In the second stage, it becomes the power of Śiva. Śiva is the innermost essence (*ātman*) of *kāla*. In the third stage *kāla* is the limiting principle, the product of *māyā* (cosmic illusion). Only in the third stage *kāla* is divided up leading to causation, duration and succession. Here the concept of *kālaśakti* covers two aspects of *Kāla* – the transcendental and the phenomenal. In Vaiṣṇava Purāṇas we sometimes come across the same theory. In *Mahābhārata* the importance of *Kāla* as *śakti* is expressed thus:

> Beyond the spirit is intelligence, beyond the intelligence Great Time (but) beyond intelligence is the Lord Viṣṇu, from whom the creation proceeds.[13] – *Gītā* X.33

The Hermeneutics of Time

With this very brief introduction about the concept of *Kāla* let me come back to the central theme of my work, viz. Bhartṛhari's conception of Time as Power. Though Time figures somewhere or the other in most of our ancient texts starting from the Vedas to Purāṇas, and in spite of the fact that it plays such an important role in Indian culture and society, surprisingly there is paucity of significant philosophical treatises that focus on *Kāla* or Time *per se*. Among the six schools of Brāhmanic philosophy, Vedānta, Sāṁkhya and Mīmāṁsā marginalize the issue. However, it is only in the fifth century CE we come across the first extant text by Bhartṛhari entirely devoted to *kāla*, entitled Kālasamuddeśa. Though Kālasamuddeśa is not a separate treatise, it forms a separate chapter (consisting of 114 *kārikās*) of the third canto of his magnum opus *Vākyapadīya*. In fact, his fascination for the

[13] Śānti-Parva, 199.2.

concept was so great that he introduces the concept in the third *kārikā* of the first canto in which he expounds his theory of linguistic non-dualism (*Śabdādvaitavāda*). Yet after that, in Indian philosophy, there is hardly any significant treatise on *kāla*. It cannot be denied that the concept of Time is supposed to find a place in all the major systems of Indian philosophy as no philosophical structure is complete without a proper explanation of the phenomenal world, be it of secondary status in the ladder of reality, or real in nature. The concept of time is essential to each philosophical system in the sense that the phenomenal world is subject to change at some basic level, i.e. production, persistence and destruction. It is the very condition of movement. All perceptible things are perceived as changing, moving, coming into existence and passing out of it. The change is also perceived to be ordered. Despite the marginalization of the concept *kāla* in classical philosophical tradition, analysis of the concept, however scanty, reveals a spectrum of views on Time. The variations in respect of this concept are indeed fascinating. On the one hand, there are realists like Nyāya-Vaiśeṣikas who emphasize the reality of Time by analysing its ontological properties such as all-pervasiveness and uniqueness, and on the other hand there are the Advaitins and Mādhyamika Buddhists, who dialectically reject the reality of Time on the ground of its phenomenal character. The status of Time in their metaphysical scheme is not only secondary but even may be said to be sub-secondary, as Śaṅkarācārya would prefer to label it as *tuccha sattā*. Again, while for some systems Time is conceived as indivisible, ubiquitous and unitary; while others project *kāla* as discreet and made of a series of atomic realities. For them all our ideas of time-continuum are mere mental constructs (*buddhi-nirmāṇa*). The conception of "time" varies depending on the metaphysical stand each school of thought adopts on such important issues as the idea of being, creation and causality. Thus an exposition of the concept of time cannot be faithfully undertaken without a look at the metaphysical position of major schools of thought. Though the central focus of my book is Bhartṛhari's theory of *Kāla* as *śakti* I would like to posit this thesis in the backdrop of two other major theories of *kāla* – Nyāya-Vaiśeṣika theory of *Kāla* as substance (*dravya*) and the Yoga and the Buddhist theory of *Kāla* as atomic continuum *(kṣaṇa/svalakṣaṇa)*. Such a study is required for placing Bhartṛhari's views on the right perspective.

Besides, we also notice that both Nyāya-Vaiśeṣika and Bhartṛhari analyse the concept of time from two dimensions – the abstract and absolute Time that is conceived as One, indivisible and all-pervading (*akhaṇḍakāla*) and the conception of divisible time that allows us to cognize, experience and speak about the empirical events in the practical level. This divisible and measurable notion of time is expressed as prior, posterior, minutes, hour, year, season and above all in the form of past, present and future. Such notions help us to put the empirical events in an orderly and harmonious way. This is called *khaṇḍakāla* (time-divided). Though the atomic theorists of Yoga and Buddhism deny the unity and indivisibility to Time in an abstract sense, it is not possible for them (or for that matter any system of thought, including Advaita Vedānta and Mādhyamika Buddhism that discard the concept as unreal) to overlook such usage, especially of past, present and future in our day-to-day language. So I have devoted a separate section for discussing the notion of *khaṇḍakāla*. This becomes evident that whatever might be the ontological scheme we cannot separate the level of metaphysics and the level of language. Another important debate that needs special attention with regard to the notion of Time is about the status of the division of Time in terms of past, present and future.

Bhartṛhari: Time, Ontology and Language

Bhartṛhari (fifth century CE) is known more as a grammarian (Vaiyākaraṇika) than a philosopher (Dārśanika). He belonged to the great grammatical and linguistic tradition of Pāṇini and Patañjali. But his three-part treatise *Vākyapadīya* (literally meaning "about sentence and the word") is much more than about grammar and sentence. It has also now been reckoned that Bhartṛhari formulated one of the first systematic forms of non-dualism, even much earlier than Śaṅkarācārya. This is evident from the fact that his *Vākyapadīya* deals more with several nuances of non-dualistic form of thought rather than explication of the rules of hermeneutics and linguistics. The first part of his treatise, that he very significantly prefers to entitle as Brahmakāṇḍa, makes his approach to his own brand of non-dualism quite clear. The metaphysical system he propounded is known as Śabdādvaitavāda that can be broadly translated as Linguistic Non-dualism – a scheme of metaphysics that ascribes the status of the Reality Supreme to *Śabda-Brahman* (that may be broadly translated as the logos or Word-principle). He systematically pursues his non-dualistic stand in the other two parts of his treatise – Vākyakāṇḍa and Prakīrnakāṇḍa. In his work he seems to present in parallel lines a philosophy of language (in the modern sense of the word) and a metaphysics of the Word that identifies *śabda-tattva* (Word-principle) with *Brahman*. Yet his contributions to both the fields of study did not receive the attention it deserved. It seems as he over-reached his limitations as a grammarian and stepped into the new arena of metaphysics, he was neglected by both, the Vyākaraṇa as well as Dārśanika traditions. The grammatical tradition ostracized him. And the philosophical tradition perhaps thought it to be below its dignity to include his work within its fold. Though Bhartṛhari's theories, especially his theory of *sphoṭa*, were debated right from Śaṅkara's to Jayanta Bhaṭṭa's works; and the great

Buddhist logician Diṅnāga used his *kārikā*s to establish his theory of meaning, his contributions in the field of philosophy was seldom recognized by the tradition of classical Indian philosophy. Moreover, unlike Śaṅkara, Bhartṛhari was not lucky enough to have any efficient disciple who could have carried on his philosophic-linguistic tradition. Puṇyarāja and Helārāja who wrote wonderful commentaries on his treatise appeared on the scene a few centuries later.

Fortunately for us the philosophical trend in the West took a "linguistic turn" during 1930s onwards with the new approach to philosophy by George Edward Moore, Bertrand Russell, Ludwig Wittgenstein and others. Philosophy centred primarily on the phenomenon called "language". This helped in a big way to resurrect Bhartṛhari. Modern Indian as well as Western scholars started taking him seriously. With the turn of the twenty-first century his place as an original thinker in the field of philosophy of language has been assured. But unfortunately, his metaphysics continues to remain, as if, a taboo. Our native scholars usually love to follow blindly the Western trend. Since metaphysics as an area of study fell from the grace in the Western philosophical tradition, we seldom focus on Bhartṛhari's metaphysical theory of Śabdādvaitavāda or the allied theories like *Kālaśakti* or *Śabdapūrvayoga*. My scanning of the entire literature on Bhartṛhari's theory of *kāla* in English made me realize that there are virtually no books in this area of study. The number of papers published in this field can be said to be negligible.

At this point I must state that Bhartṛhari's philosophy of language and his metaphysics of linguistic non-dualism cannot be segregated. They are intricately interwoven. One is incomplete without the other. For example, to have a real grasp of his now famous theory of *sphoṭa* one needs to know about the theory of *śabdatattva Brahman*. Similarly, to know about how the language functions in the practical level (*lokavyavahāra*) we need to know his theory of *kāla* and *krama*. This is evident from Bhartṛhari's work. Though he exclusively deals with *kāla* in the 9th section of the Prakīrnakāṇḍa (IIIrd canto), the idea of *Kāla* as the power of *Śabda-Brahman* was introduced in the third *kārikā* of the Brahmakāṇḍa (Ist canto) itself, the part which also deals with his philosophy of language. In fact, the first three *kārikā*s of the first canto make one aware of Bhartṛhari's unflinching absolutistic and non-dualistic stance, both, in the level of language as well as in the level of metaphysics.

Kāla plays such an important role in his metaphysical scheme, for like all other metaphysical systems (especially non-dualism), Bhartṛhari has the compulsion to elucidate the relation between the transcendental, One, unique and timeless Reality (*Brahman*) on the one hand, and the phenomenal world characterized by change and diversity, on the other. Similarly, Bhartṛhari has to justify the relation between the ultimate unity of the linguistic potency (*sphoṭa*) and the diversities of its manifestations in the spoken or phonetic level. In both the levels it is a shift from the sequenceless to the sequential. In the level of linguistic communication, uttered and written language is exclusively sequential in nature; similarly, in the phenomenal level the world (*jagata*) is characterized by processes (*prakriyā*) (that too is sequential). It is a shift from the changeless to changing; and from unity to diversity. Therein lie the significance of *Kāla* as a concept. So in this work I have tried my best to place his Theory of Time in both the levels – ontological and linguistic.

Besides, Śabdādvaitavāda of Bhartṛhari as one of the earliest systematic Advaita theory must be compared and contrasted with the Advaitavāda of Śaṅkara. There are certain questions that are likely to bother us once Bhartṛhari's metaphysics is taken seriously. For example can we compare Bhartṛhari's idea of *Kālaśakti* with Śaṅkara's *māyā*? Do they use the term *avidyā* in the same sense? Both of them talk of

Vivarttavāda. Are these terms used with the same connotation? There are plethora of such interesting issues that, if investigated, would make the study of Indian philosophical tradition more invigorating.

2

The Metaphysics of the Word
Bhartṛhari on Śabdādvaitavāda

MAN is always in search of a better consistency and clarity in his framework of thought. Understood in this sense, metaphysics as an intellectual pursuit does not aim at solving the mysteries of the trans-empirical realities. It is another name for thought that seeks self-consistency. So, metaphysics as an intellectual pursuit does not primarily signify investigation into ontology, but an analysis of certain basic concepts, that is characterized by a better power, offers a consistent view of life and the universe. For a philosopher concepts are the tools through which he wishes to explain two basic perplexities that he faces in the world of the irremediable flow of sensations. They are plurality and change. These two features that he encounters in day-to-day life need to be explained and systematized. He is in the quest for a systematic and consistent conceptual framework in which the chaotic dimensions of experience are fitted in. This consistency comes from the human propensity for rationality. However we must remember that the postulates that a metaphysician holds close to his heart can neither be proved nor disproved. They are simply postulates; and in their manipulation of concepts sometimes philosophers rely on this or that concept heavily. They pull this or that string of the conceptual net and the net appears in this or that shape. We may label this tendency of the metaphysicians, a form of "intellectual imperialism" following Strawson.[1] Thus the philosophers have a tendency to produce strikingly different world-picture dominated by a specific concept, representing a particular attitude or interest. If the non-dualist puts stress on the concept of "unity" then the pluralists sees more rationality in the concept of "plurality". Accordingly they present the rational and conceptual scheme in such a way that everything suits the scheme of concepts. I have already stated in the introductory chapter that Time or *kāla* is a concept that the Indian metaphysicians use to elucidate – how they want to look at the human life, his experience and the world at large? Depending on their scheme of thought in this regard either they deny the reality to *kāla* and just relegate it to the position of a subjective phenomenon or ascertain its importance as a reality. So without delving into Bhartṛhari's metaphysics we shall not be in a position to truly assess why he conceives *Kāla* as a *śakti*. In this chapter I would therefore try to provide an outline of his metaphysics famously known as Śabdādvaitavāda.

Śabda as Brahman

We know that in the last few decades philosophers have been fascinated by the concept of language and this obsession with the concept has almost become the occupational disease of the modern philosophers. Yet nowhere in the history of ideas we come across a system of thought entirely structured around the concept of *śabda* (Word). The philosophical position presented by the fifth century grammarian–philosopher Bhartṛhari not only presents a strikingly distinctive picture of the word and the world, but makes us realize the importance of the phenomenon called language. In the classical Indian tradition, however, the concept of language has always played an important role in the philosophical quest. In fact, the

---

1 Strawson 1992: 14.

inquisitiveness about "language" as a concept is as old as the Indian civilization itself. This is evident from the fact that *Ṛgveda*, the oldest scripture of India, contains innumerable insightful remarks about the nature of *śabda* (language) and *vāk* (speech). This fascination was more articulately presented in the philosophical scriptures and texts of the subsequent period. Most of the philosophical traditions took up the problem of language as a part of their epistemological concern, otherwise known as Pramāṇaśāstra. But in Bhartṛhari's case the analysis of *śabda* goes beyond the limits of Pramāṇaśāstra. He was in the true sense of the term the first philosopher of language in India, who dared to develop a metaphysics based on the famous Upaniṣadic line – *vāk vai Brahman* (Word/the principle of speech is verily *Brahman*[2]). His very comprehensive inquiry about the nature of language ultimately culminates in the idea of a linguistic non-dualism (Śabdādvaita). It is a form of non-dualism in which the principle of language (*śabdatattva*) is identified with *Brahman*. With this brief introduction about Bhartṛhari I shall like to go straight into his Theory of Linguistic Non-dualism.

Let me now try to explicate in brief the Bhartṛharian metaphysics centred on the concept of *śabdopagrāhī* with the help of a seminal verse that occurs in the opening stanza of the first canto (Brahmakāṇḍa) of *Vākyapadīya*. He declares:

anādi nidhanaṁ brahma śabdatattvaṁ yadakṣaram ।
vivartate arthabhāvena prakriyā jagato yataḥ ॥

These lines can be translated in the following way:

> The *Brahman* is without beginning and end, whose essence is the Word (also translated as Word-essence, *Eternal verbum*) who is the cause of the manifested phonemes (speech), who appears (*vivartate*) as the objects (*artha*), from whom the activities of the world proceed (*jagato prakriyā*).

---

2 *Bṛhadāraṇyaka Upanisad* 4.1.2.

Anybody acquainted with the Upaniṣadic and Advaitin traditions may not feel much uncomfortable with the first half of the verse. *Brahman* in such traditions is presented as eternal, all-pervading and without change; hence without beginning and end. But ambiguity seems to creep in once we come across the line "the Word-essence appears as objects and from whom the activities of the world proceed". This line at first glance seems mystical and also very uncritical. Yet this second half of the verse is most crucial for understanding the basic philosophical position of Bhartṛhari. Let us, therefore explicate what Bhartṛhari exactly seems to imply by the second half of the *kārikā*. I feel that the clue to understand the above-mentioned line rests on our grasping of the word *śabdatattva-Brahman*.

Very broadly understood, *śabda* means sound. If we go for still more strict interpretation then *śabda* should mean "written or uttered string of sounds with syntax and also meaning". This is the sense in which the term *śabda-pramāṇa* has been used by most of the philosophical systems in India. But for Bhartṛhari the term *śabda* has a still more deep implication. It is the name of a complex phenomenon implying an activity as well as a principle. As an activity it is something in which all human beings are engaged. This activity is guided by particularized speech pattern having syntax, meaning and expressing the intention of the speaker. The Sanskrit term that Bhartṛhari uses for this activity is *śabdanā vyāpāra*. Following B.K. Matilal we may translate it as "languageing".[3] In this case *śabda* stands for a string of sounds having syntax and also meaning. It is called an activity as human beings are engaged in exchange of thoughts and experiences with one another through the use of language. Again *śabda*, according to Bhartṛhari, may stand for a principle. This is unitary in nature, and the potential

---

3 Matilal 1990: 85.

ground of all our conscious activities, including thought, conceptualization, speech and our awareness of the phenomenal world. This principle of language is called the Word-essence (*śabda-tattva*). This is identified with *Brahman*, the highest Reality. We know that in our Upaniṣadic tradition the highest Reality is called *Brahman*. Etymologically speaking, the term *Brahman* is derived from the root *vṛḥ* that means, "to grow, to expand, to become great". In extended sense, therefore, *Brahman* means "an all-pervading principle". Now we may infer that why for Bhartṛhari *śabda-tattva* (Word-principle) is also *Brahman*? *Śabdatattva* as a principle pervades our thought, cognition, awareness and consciousness of the phenomenal world. So this all-pervading unitary principle is called *Śabda-Brahman*.

The Word and the World

Even if we take it for granted that *śabdatattva-Brahman* is the highest Reality, does it not look incongruous to claim that *śabdatattva-Brahman* "appears as objects and all the phenomenal activities proceed from this". Unless Bhartṛhari convincingly explains the logical and conceptual connection between the empirical world characterized by objects and activities, on the one hand, and the Reality Supreme that is of the nature of the Word, on the other, his metaphysical system is likely to collapse. So let us explore and examine Bhartṛhari's own justifications for the claim.

We all know that the world of objects does not have anything common with the world of words. Objects are believed to be out there and we apply words to refer to them. But in his explanatory note on the verse mentioned above Bhartṛhari provides an altogether different interpretation of "objects". He says objects are *śabdopagrāhī*. In other words, objects are word-determined. Be it perception, inference or any other method, whenever we cognize as objects we do so in terms of names. On the basis of names we identify objects and distinguish one class of objects from another. So we use names or particular words to mean a particular object. If objects are not nameable they are not identifiable, hence not cognizable. Our cognition on the other hand is *śabdopagrāhya*, i.e. word-impregnated or intertwined with words. Our consciousness and cognition have a natural potency to act through words. We know that cognitions belong to the level of thought which is distinct from our speech. But our thought itself is intertwined with word-potency, for we think and conceptualize in terms of words. In other words, the objects of our thought, too has to be nameable. Thus both cognition and objects, being word-generated, are in principle, dependent on *śabda Brahman*.

Regarding this unusual theory about the word–world relationship Bhartṛhari offers further justifications. He argues that the objects are identified as distinct objects once they are subsumed under a word or a name. Otherwise, the world of objects is unidentifiable and indistinguishable "something". In other words, distinction is made between one object and another on the basis of words or names assigned to them. According to Bhartṛhari the phenomenal world in which live and experience is a matter of how we know it and cognize it. All sorts of knowledge, including our awareness of facts, are possible because we assign a name (*nāma*) and form (*rūpa*) to the objects and processes of the world. We think, conceptualize and become conscious of everything through our potential to associate them with words or names. Such awareness of the names and forms of the phenomenal world finally is expressed through the language that helps us to communicate with one another and form a human society. So man is not only a thinking and cognizing being but he is primarily a languageing being. Take away the word (names and concepts) man would be nothing more than a lifeless log of wood;[4] again without word-generated names the world is reduced to a confused mass. Thus we notice that the word *śabda*, for Bhartṛhari has two dimensions – as *śabdatattva*, this is the root of all human activity including his awareness of his own existence; and again *śabda* in the particularized form is the very basis of man's cognition and linguistic communication. In this sense, *Śabda* (Word-essence) is the all-pervading. *Śabda* as *tattva* (principle) is the very ground of understanding and mapping of the phenomenal world. So *Śabda-Brahman* is the ultimate ground of the phenomenal world.

This theory of Bhartṛhari is in direct contrast to the Nyāya view about the cognition of objects. Gotama in his *Nyāya-Sūtra* (I.I.4) states non-verbalizability (*avyapadeśya*) as one of the characteristics of our cognition of objects. Elaborating this point Vātsyāyana adds that our perception need not be always associated with verbalization, and there can always be non-linguistic cognition (*nirvikalpa pratyakṣa*). So verbalization is not a condition of our cognition of the objects and the world. In support of his argument he cites the examples of a mute's or a child's perception. Bhartṛhari had already anticipated this objection. He says that even a mute's or a child's cognition is not without the element of the potency for verbalization. He clarifies that there can be two types of words – articulate words that are speakable and non-articulate words that are unspeakable.[5] Non-articulate words refer to the linguistic potency of a child, for their actions are prompted by language.[6] In other words, a child may not be in a position to verabalize but that does not imply the absence of linguistic potency in them. In short, "verbalization" and "verbalizabilty" are not identical concepts.

---

4 *VP* I.127.

5 *ākhyeyarūpanām anākhyeya rūpanām ca śabdānām – VP,* Vṛtti under I.113.

6 *anākhyeya-śabdanibandha bālānam pravṛtti* – ibid.

Our perceptual cognition need not be always articulated in verbal form. But that does not preclude the possibility of the potency for linguistic expressibility. In case of a mute, the element of speech is not absolutely absent. Bhartṛhari specifies:

> (S)peech inheres in all cases of awareness just as illumination does in fire and consciousness in the mind. The subtle nature of *vāc* (speech) penetrates and permeates even such states as lack of ostensive mental activity. . . .[7]

Even the bare awareness of objects (*nirvikalpa pratyakṣa*) is not possible without their being potent with cognitive discrimination (*pratyavamarśa*).[8] When we fail to subsume the cognition of an object under a name, we understand it with the help of the words "this" or "that". Therefore, without cognitive discrimination there is no object. Such discrimination is possible through conceptualization; and conceptualization is penetrated (*aṇuviddha*) by the word. Bhartṛhari makes it clear:

> There is no cognition in the world in which the word does not figure. All knowledge is as it were intertwined with the word.[9]

Here Bhartṛhari differs from the Nyāya way of delineating the world and the objects. Nyāya metaphysics adopts a realistic and pluralistic stand that accords reality to the phenomenal world independent of mind and consciousness. Bhartṛhari,

---

7 *VP, Vṛtti* under I.124.

8 *vāgrūpatāced utkrāmed avabodhasya śaśvatī* ।
na prakāśaḥ prakāśeta sā hi pratyavamarśini ॥ – *VP* I.124

If the eternal identity of knowledge and word is taken away, knowledge would cease to be knowledge. It is the identity which makes the identity possible.

9 *na so 'sti pratyayo loke yaḥ śabdānugamād ṛte* ।
anubiddhamiva jñānaṁ sarvaṁ śabdena bhāsate ॥ – *VP* I.123

on the other hand, is an idealist and non-dualist. For him, the phenomenal world is known because the mind is conscious of it and consciousness is nothing but word-potent.

The second argument that Bhartṛhari advances in support of his thesis comes from the logic of causality (especially, Satkāryavāda) prevalent in the ancient Indian tradition. Such a theory of causality takes it for granted that the properties of cause continue in the effects or in the manifestations. Therefore, on the basis of observation of the nature of effects we can infer the cause. For example, the curd as the effect of milk retains some of the qualities of milk. On the basis of these qualities one can infer that milk is the cause of the curd, not the water. Similarly, on the basis of observation of the word-potent nature of the phenomenal world we can infer that the cause of the world is the Word. On this basis Bhartṛhari declares:

> It is the word, which sees the object, it is the word, which speaks, it is the word, which reveals the object, which was lying hidden, and it is on the word that the multiple world rests.[10]

In the above passage the objects are said to be "lying hidden", because, according to him the objects may exist *ad libitum*, but their true nature is not known unless and until they are subsumed under some names. This is evident from the following argument of Bhartṛhari:

> Even that exists is as good as non-existent as long as it does not come within the range of verbal usage. Even totally non-existent things like hare's horn or something which appears and disappears in the sky like celestial town (*gandhava nagara*) when brought in to mind by word figures like something endowed with primary Reality, in various usages.[11]

---

10 *VP*, *Vṛtti* under I.118.

11 *VP*, *Vṛtti* under I.121.

This passage to a large extent clarifies Bhartṛhari's position on world–Word relationship. The function of the word is to "mean"; but to mean is not to refer to an existent object. It is not a relation that can be stated in "Fido"-Fido mould, i.e. here is the word 'Fido', and there is the dog Fido. In Bhartṛhari's metaphysical scheme there is no duality between the level of facts and the level of language. These two levels are non-differentiable as objects are only analysable through language. The world of objects and the world of words cannot be cognized independent of one another. In Bhartṛhari's auto-commentary on the above *kārikā* he explains, "it appears as objects", is this – what is called appearance (*vivartta*) is the assumption by the One, without losing its oneness through apparent diversity, of unreal forms of others. It has been said:

> The spatial and temporal manifestations are no more than functioning of the power of Nescience, they are neither identical nor different from the one, which is Truth.[12]

So from the word-potent nature all that is there in the empirical world the non-duality of the *Śabda-Brahman* is established. The diversities according to him are unreal. It is *vivartta;* hence does not have the reality in the ontological sense. Further, *Śabda-Brahman* is without inner sequence, undifferentiated and inexpressible.

Nature of the World

With this way of interpreting the relation between the word and the world, Bhartṛhari exhibits how there is a constant interplay between the unity and diversity. But unity is always the real/primary, for, without the assumption of the unity, diversity is not possible. Unity itself is the potential ground of the diversity. Though in the level of use there is distinction between the concept and percept, speech and thought, concepts

---

12 Tr. Iyer, *Vṛtti* under I.1.

and identifiable names, they all merge together, as if, in the womb of the potency called *śabda*. But thereby, Bhartṛhari is not presenting a form of nominalism. The world for him is not a concatenation of names. The world exists but it is never cognizable as such, but always through the "cloak" of words. In other words, he steers clear of referential theory of meaning favoured by the Nyāya school of philosophy. He is not willing to accept the dictum that language pictures the reality. Bhartṛhari, of course, has some cogent arguments in support of his thesis. He points out:

> It is extremely difficult to establish by reasoning the nature of objects, because their properties differ according to differences in circumstances, place and time.[13]

So what we usually call as the "world" or a "fact" has only metaphorical existence (*upacāra sattā*). If it can ever be known it is only through the attributes superimposed on it. And such attributes are due to our conceptualization made possible through the power of language. This position of Bhartṛhari is nothing unusual. We may note that the famous Western philosopher Immanuel Kant places a similar view. For him too the world as such is unknown and unknowable. Whatever we know about the experienceable world is arranged and systemized by the categories of thought/understanding. But Bhartṛhari being a linguistic non-dualist would say that even the categories of thought are word-determined. That is the exact reason why he uses the word *vivartate* (appears), i.e. *vivartate arthabhāvena*, in the second line of the verse quoted in the beginning of this chapter. The objects are not the real transformation of the Word-principle but apparent transformation. Thus, so far as Bhartṛhari's philosophy is concerned, there is no real gap between thought, world and language. They all are penetrated by the Word-principle. As

13 *VP* I.32.

a self-proclaimed philosopher of language (*śabda-pramāṇaka*) this is the only consistent way to explain the relation between the world and the word. For a philosopher of language what the word presents is the only method of understanding the Reality. So he explicitly declares: *arthaścāsmākam yaḥ śabdenābhidhīyate* (object for us is what the word presents).[14]

Śabda and Linguistic Communication

Thus we find that Bhartṛhari very cogently establishes why he holds that *śabda* or the Word is the ground of the world. But he carries on his analysis of the phenomenon called *śabda* in another level. This level is sometimes described as *vyāpāra*, and sometimes as *lokavyavahāra*. This is the level in which language is seen as an activity of human communication. For him language is not a set of sterile symbols but a social phenomenon. This is a communicative tool and social phenomenon. In this level too Bhartṛhari highlights on the interplay between diversity and unity. In this case also, unity is more real than diversity. The same *Śabda-Brahman* as *Śabdatattva* (principle of speech) reflects the same pattern – a movement from unity to diversity. *Śabda* stands for the potential ground of all our linguistic activity in the form of speech. It is manifested in diverse concepts and linguistic forms to find final expression in the form of uttered words.

We may agree with Bhartṛhari that without the word there is no thought, no awareness, no cognition and no knowledge of the existence of the phenomenal world as such. But is it not a fact that our thoughts and words could be episodic? They can be many. To answer this pertinent question we have to delve a bit on his conception of language itself. Bhartṛhari makes a clear-cut distinction between the three levels of understanding the concept of *śabda*. *Śabda* could be seen as a principle (*śabdatattva*), it too could be explored in the level of

---

[14] Bhartṛhari 1967: 298.

language-in-use which he calls as *lokavyavahāra*, and finally *śabda* could also be an object of analytical and grammatical study (*śāstravyavahāra*). When language is seen from the angle of communicative use it involves several factors. In case of any linguistic communication, we have to presume three important elements: (a) speaker; (b) hearer; and (c) a common ground between the speaker and the hearer. Again, in case of the speaker who linguistically expresses some thought through utterance there are three concepts involved, viz. the meaning (*vācya*), the string of word (*vācaka*), and the intention of the speaker (*vivakṣā*). When the speaker intends to mean something he uses the utterances that convey a sense. Though analytically speaking one may distinguish between the words (or sound pattern) and meaning, but in the level of its use unless they are seen as unitary the words would fail to express a sense. In this case Bhartṛhari brings to notice one of the peculiar features of the level of utterance. It is sequential (*krama*) by nature. The moment a syllable is uttered, it is replaced by another syllable. So the speaker expresses whatever he has to say with the help of sequences of syllables. The hearer too grasps the sense conveyed to him by the speaker through such sequential order. Bhartṛhari very emphatically points out:

> And nothing can be expressed through the words which has not assumed sequence.[15]

Despite such sequential grasping of words, the hearer grasps the meaning as one whole as he is endowed with the linguistic potency (*śabda bhāvanā*). According to Bhartṛhari the hearer does not add up the series of words and its meanings to understand what the speaker intends to mean. The sense is understood as a unitary whole. When *X* says "I am hungry" the hearer does not keep on adding up the meaning of the individual words to understand the utterance. He immediately

---

[15] *VP* I.186.

grasps the unitary sense conveyed by the sequential string of sounds. In the speaker's case also there is a notion of unity involved. Though the speaker utters words in sequence what he intends to express is a unitary sense. But it might be asked – how does the speaker manage to convey the meaning that has a unitary sense? Bhartṛhari's answer to the question is quite interesting, yet profound. We do not come across such a cogent account of the process of linguistic communication either in Indian philosophical tradition or in the modern Western philosophy of language. According to him our level of utterance is like the tip of the iceberg. It is only the last stage of the process of linguistic communication, which he names as the *vaikharī vāk* (articulated speech). The level of utterance points to a deeper level, viz. thought.

I have already discussed how Bhartṛhari emphasizes that thought is not possible without the elements of linguistic potency. The gap that is sometimes maintained between the level of speech and the level of thought merges in case of linguistic communication, for, in order to communicate the speaker needs to have an "intention" to express a sense. Similarly, the hearer, on his part has to "understand" or "grasp" the sense intended for communication by the speaker. Both, the "intention" of the speaker as well as the "understanding of the hearer automatically point to a level beyond speech. This is the level of thought which Bhartṛhari calls it *madhyamā vāk*. "Mind is its only substratum."[16] This is an unexpressed pre-verbal stage. It is a stage with the same verbal contents. The sequence is also implicitly present in the *madhyamā vāk*. This pre-verbal stage further points to a deeper level – called *paśyantī vāk* – the pure non-verbal stage of language. This is the stage in which the potency for the expressiveness is inherent. It stands for a non-differentiated

---

16 *VP*, *Vṛtti* under I.142.

principle and is identical with consciousness. So we notice how Bhartṛhari unfolds that in the level of ordinary speech too there is a movement from the diversity to unity; from differentiated to undifferentiated.

The Problem of Unity and Diversity

Bhartṛhari's explication of how the language operates in the level of *lokavyavahāra* would be incomplete if we do not attend to another important issue, i.e. how the sense is conveyed by the speaker to the hearer? Is it like transporting the contents of one wagon from another? But in that case human language would turn into a mechanical process. It would no longer be a human affair. So we have to assume a common ground that is shared by both, the speaker and the hearer. The meaning that is expressed by particular a sentence or word cannot be said to present the meaning as a whole. The particularized expression of a "sense" or a "meaning" through a sentence or a word can at best give us a "piece" or a "bit" of the linguistic-whole. For example, "I am hungry" – here "I" or "hungry" can have multiple connotations; the same word can express different meanings depending on the context; similarly the same sense can be expressed in more than one way. So when we use language for communication we extract a "part" from this whole on the basis of what we intend to express. This is done by the method of what Bhartṛhari calls as *apoddhāra*, i.e. "the process of constant and progressive extraction, comparison and abstraction". The meaning is attached to this abstracted bits from the linguistic-whole (or meaning-whole) by abstracting letter from words, words from sentences, sentences from discourse, discourse from the larger discourses till we refer to the ultimate point of our linguistic potency (that is sometimes also variously called as the "real-word", "linguistic-whole" or "the meaning-whole"). Bhartṛhari calls this ultimate merging point as *sphoṭa*. It is the *sphoṭa* which is posited as the common ground between the speaker and the hearer. The differentiation between the speaker's meaning and the hearer's meaning is obliterated because they share the common *sphoṭa*.

It is very difficult to translate the term *sphoṭa* for no translation can be adequate enough to bring out the real implication of the word *sphoṭa*. The word is derived from the root *sphuṭ*, which means bursting forth. So by implication we may say that *sphoṭa* stands for the meaning-whole from which the meaning and the sense expressed as if bursts forth along with phonetic and syntactic elements. Without going into the details of the concept, let us for the time-being highlight on the nature of the *sphoṭa*. For Bhartṛhari *sphoṭa* is the operative ground of our linguistic communication. This concept is a pivotal point of his analysis of what do we do with the words. We know that language has multiple nuances and we use it in unlimited number of ways to express our thought. Not only the speaker but the hearer too has the capability to understand and interpret them in similar fashion. This is possible because all language-using beings have the unitary linguistic potency. This is the non-differentiated ground of words, meaning and the object-meant. So each episodic expression is nothing but only a part of the expressible meaning-whole. This not only applies to episodic thought but the human being's ability for linguistic communication. Though Bhartṛhari never explicitly associates *paśyantī vāk* with *sphoṭa* we can infer this from his commentary on I.142. It is stated herein:

> The seeing one (*paśyantī*) is that in which sequence is merged and though it is One *the power to produce sequence* has entered into it.

Again, *paśyantī* is also described as restless. This nature points to its potency to manifest itself in preverbal and non-verbal stage. Understood in this sense, we can be in a better position to understand Bhartṛhari's illustration that the potency of language is like a pea-hen's egg. All the colours of the fully grown pea-hen is potentially there in the egg. These colours are manifested when the pea-hen comes out of the egg. Similarly, *sphoṭa, śabda* and *paśyantī vāk,* all such concepts refer to the potential state in which the linguistic form along with its power to mean is already there in all languageing beings.[17] Elaborating the three stages of the linguistic process (*vaikharī, madhyamā* and *paśyantī*) Bhartṛhari says:

> All objects (meant) merge into intellect (as potentialities) and intellect merges into sequenceless Word as potentiality.[18]

Similarly, we use language to refer to the objects. I have already stated that Bhartṛhari does not subscribe to a referential theory of meaning, i.e. words do not directly refer to the objects. The world of objects as such is not knowable. Whatever we know of objects is limited by concepts – the linguistic constructs (*vikalpa*). The concepts involve the process of selection and elimination. For example, the word *ghaṭa* (pot) as a concept may signify the universal of *ghataṭva* (potness). But the particular of the pot referred to can be described and meant in innumerable ways. We can refer to pot's colour by saying "the pot is red", or else we refer to its shape we can as well say, "the pot is round", and so on. Thus the whole of the object-meant can never be grasped by language. The same object can be meant differently with reference to different words that express it differently. In each case we present a limited and selected aspect of it. Thus the "whole of the meaning-expressed" and the "whole of the object-meant" are non-graspable by the "bits" of linguistic units. So we come to a position where we note that, for Bhartṛhari, "language", "thought" and "reality" (the objects-meant) refer to a point of unity. Bhartṛhari would say that this unitary whole is nothing

---

17 *VP* I.51.

18 *VP, Vṛtti* on I.118.

but the meaning-whole (*sphoṭa*) or what Matilal translates as the non-differentiated language-principle.[19] This is shared by both, the speaker and the hearer so that human beings can communicate what they are capable of thinking and speaking meaningfully. This potency is one and non-differentiated but becomes differentiated when it is manifested by particularized expressions of thought and intention.

The Problem of Change

I have mentioned at the outset that philosopher's main concern is to disentangle two perplexing phenomena that are the benchmarks of the phenomenal world, viz. diversity and change. Bhartṛhari in accordance with his non-dualistic approach has very coherently shown how the One and unique *Śabda-Brahman* could accommodate the diversity. But the problem that needs to be addressed is about the phenomenon called change. He has already proclaimed that the Reality is unchangeable and is non-sequential. The phenomenal world being characterized by change owes an explanation in terms of the unchangeable Reality. To address this issue Bhartṛhari introduces the concept of *Kāla*. As all our cognitions, experience and awareness about the world are word-potent, they are conceivable and communicable in terms language. But one of the atypical features of language-in-use is its sequential nature. Similarly, all our experiences, be it of the external world or inner states of mind, such as pleasure and pain are arranged in time in a sequential manner (*krama*). Otherwise we cannot distinguish one experience from the other. Sequence implies change. So he uses two concepts – sequence (*krama*) and action (*kriyā*) – to elucidate the phenomenal world. Both the concepts are the very ground of understanding the notion of change. Like the other Advaitins, Bhartṛhari could have avoided the problem of "change". He has already established his non-

[19] Matilal 1990: 85.

dualistic credentials by elaborating how the One and unique *Brahman*, could be transformed into the diversity of the *jagat* (phenomenal world). But Bhartṛhari offers equal attention to the problem of change. So he takes recourse to elevate *Kāla* as a power of *Brahman* to explain both, the diversity and change that pervades the empirical world; both in the level of facts and in the level of linguistic use. He exhibits very convincingly the transition from diversity to unity, and from sequentiality/changeability to non-sequentiality/unchangeability.

3

Time as Power: Bhartṛhari

We have noted in the previous chapter that according to Bhartṛhari, the reality of the phenomenal world, including the objects of experience, cognition, perception as well as awareness of them, everything is but a manifestation of the Word-essence (*Śabdatattva-Brahman*). Herein the concept of time comes in as the main conceptual tool that facilitates his metaphysics of linguistic non-dualism. In this chapter, I would like to examine in detail Bhartṛhari's analysis of the concept of *Kāla* as a conceptual apparatus. I have stated earlier, he exclusively deals with the concept of *Kāla* in a separate chapter entitled Kālasamuddeśa in the third canto of *Vākyapadīya*. This section contains 114 *kārikā*s. We are not sure whether he ever wrote the *vṛtti*s of these *kārikā*s, as is claimed in case of the first canto of his treatise. But Helārāja (CE 1050–1100), the renowned follower of his tradition, composed a detailed explanatory commentary of the third canto entitled Prakīrṇa(ka) Prakāśa. The cryptic *kārikā*s of Kālasamuddeśa would have remained vague without Helārāja's *vṛtti*. So I shall primarily depend on Helārāja's commentary while explicating Bhartṛhari's theory of *Kāla*.

Kāla: The Metaphysical Background

Before we take up a detailed discussion on Bhartṛhari's conception of *Kāla* as a *śakti* let us have a brief perusal of the possible sources of this novel concept. We already know that Bhartṛhari did not belong to any of the six systems of the

Brāhmanical–philosophical streams. He proclaimed himself to be a follower of the great grammatical tradition propounded by Pāṇini and Patañjali. But in the previous chapter, I have already discussed how he weaves a metaphysical theory around the concept of *śabda*. The very idea of Śabdādvaita was novel in the sense that the concept of *śabda*, though discussed in the classical systems of Indian philosophy, was never taken to the limelight so as to be transformed into the Reality Supreme. Once Bhartṛhari projects *Śabdatattva-Brahman* as the pivot, he has the metaphysical compulsion to introduce some more original concepts to make his metaphysical superstructure secure. So the very idea of elevating Time as a principal concept seems more as a link in the chain of his non-dualistic metaphysics than the continuation of any specific tradition, be it of the Vaiyākaraṇikas or of the Dārśanikas. His originality lies in developing a metaphysical as well as a linguistic scheme that centres on the concept *Kāla* which helps him to elaborate the theme of unity and diversity, both, in the level of linguistic usage as well as in the abstract level of ontology.

What makes his theory more fundamental is the fact that one virtually does not come across any systematic account of such an important metaphysical concept like "time" prior to him. There are stray references to this notion in *Atharvaveda, Maitrāyaṇī Upaniṣad* and some epics like *Mahābhārata*. So what could have inspired Bhartṛhari to formulate the theory of *Kālaśakti*? Was it the Grammatical tradition? Let us then scan the comments and opinions of his predecessors like Pāṇini, Patañjali and Kaiyaṭa to trace the source of the theory of *Kāla* as *śakti*, for in no accredited system of Indian philosophy *Kāla* is labelled as *śakti*. One of the earliest of definition of the concept of Time comes from Pāṇini (500 BCE), whose *sūtra* reads *kālaḥ parimāṇinā*. This *sūtra* provides some profound insights regarding time or the uses of the temporal words.

Commentators like Patañjali and Kaiyaṭa have discussed the *sūtra* at greater length and advanced some crucial suggestions regarding the import of the word *Kāla*. Patañjali's discussions on the idea of *Kāla,* however brief, adumbrates the distinction between Time as an all-pervading continuous flow and the measurable time. In this context, Patañjali's commentaries (*bhāṣya*) on Pāṇini's *sūtra*s, entitled *Mahābhāṣya,* is of some help in assessing Bhartṛhari's position vis-à-vis *Kālaśakti.* Patañjali explicitly admits the eternality of Time. Under Pāṇini's rule IV.2.3, he states that both time and stars are eternal.[1] Not only time is eternal, but in his estimation time is the ultimate substratum of the universe (*kālohi jagaddhāraḥ*). He regards Time as indivisible, permanent, one and all-pervading. Accordingly he defines time as that whereby the growth and decay of the material objects are perceived.[2] Kaiyaṭa elaborates it further by saying:

> Now we see development, now decay in things such as creeper, trees; other causes remaining the same. This change (*pariṇāma*) is due to time.[3]

However, Patañjali makes it clear that this eternal Time is not to be confused with the temporal measures such as day and night, months and years. In his opinion, such divisions of time are only artificial calculations. This is due to its conjunction with some actions as movement of the sun (*kāyakriyāya ādityagatya*).[4] In fact, Patañjali provides quite interesting insights on different dimensions of time, including the nature of three basic divisions of time into past, present and future. Now it

---

1 *nityehi kālanakṣatre – Mahābhāṣya on Pāṇini* IV.2.3

2 *yena mūrtināṁ upacayaścāpacayaśca lakṣyante tam kālam āhu – Mahābhāṣya on Pāṇini* II.2.5.

3 Kaiyaṭa, *Pradīpa* on *Mahābhāṣya on Pāṇini* II.2.5.

4 *Mahābhāṣya on Pāṇini* II.2.5.

may seem obvious that Bhartṛhari draws his inspiration, largely, from Patañjali's commentaries, as would be unfolded during the detailed discussion on his conception of *Kālaśakti*. At the same time it must be made clear that Patañjali was not the only thinker to hold that Time is eternal; and temporal measurements are artificial. Vaiśeṣika too shares this stand as is obvious from the frequent reference to this system in Bhartṛhari's Kālasamuddeśa. But the originality of his approach lies in elevating *Kāla* to the status of the *śakti* (power) of *Brahman*. In this context it should be noted that Patañjali never makes it clear whether he considers *Kāla* as a substance or as a power. So the idea of *Kāla* as *śakti* is not directly drawn from Patañjali. To seek the alternative sources that might have inspired Bhartṛhari's idea let us turn to Purāṇas. No doubt, some of the Śaiva Purāṇas-like ideas such as *Rūdra Saṁhitā* and *Vāyavīya Saṁhitā* portray *Kāla* as the energy of Śiva, the highest Reality in their ontological scheme. But we cannot come to hasty conclusion that the concept of *Kāla* as *śakti* is borrowed from Śaiva-Purāṇas. There are certain basic differences between Bhartṛhari's idea of *Kālaśakti* and the Śaiva theory of *Kāla*. While the Śaivādvaita theories speak of Time as the power of God, one does not come across any reference to any personal God in Bhartṛhari's theory. *Kāla* is rather conceived as the power of the impersonal, *Śabdatattva-Brahman*. He, in all respects, follows the Upaniṣadic non-dualism that is not so prominently reflected in the Śaiva Āgamas. So, we cannot exactly trace the source of his theory of *Kālaśakti* in any Purāṇic tradition. There is every possibility that his approach to non-dualism from parallel angles – as a linguist as well as a metaphysician – might have led him to introduce this innovative idea. This may become obvious from the three introductory *kārikā*s of the first canto of his *Vākyapadīya*, as well as the auto-commentaries.

The Concept of Śakti

As we have noted in the last chapter, the first verse of *Vākyapadīya* introduces three important concepts – *Śabdatattva* as *Brahman* (Word-principle), *jagat prakriyā* (processes of the world) and *vivartta* (evolution). I have also discussed how and why *Śabdatattva-Brahman* is accorded the status of the Reality Supreme. Now let us take a note of another important concept that could be derived from the first *kārikā*, viz. *prakriyā jagato yataḥ*, i.e. process of the world. The use of this word "process" makes it explicit that Bhartṛhari delineates the world as something dynamic and subject to continuous change. In his autocommentary on this *kārikā* he writes:

> All objects through their *beginning, sustenance* and *end* can be determined only through words. [italics mine]

Thus, we can infer that according to him the Reality (*Śabda-Brahman*) evolves (*vivartate*) as the processes of the world from the initial beginning (*sṛṣṭi*) to the final re-absorption (*saṁhāra*). So the first *kārikā* itself offers us a clear picture about why he holds the concept of Time as an important conceptual tool without which the link between the *jagat prakriyā* and Reality Supreme *Śabdatattva-Brahman* would be snapped.

In the very next *kārikā* he brings in another important notion, viz. *śakti*:

> Who has been taught as the One appearing as many due to multiplicity of his powers [*śakti*], who, though, non-different from his powers, seem to be so. – tr. K.A.S. Iyer

In this *kārikā* we come across the word *śakti*. It is important to note that Bhartṛhari uses the word *śakti* not only in the context of metaphysics, but other contexts too. As our chief concern here is to comprehend how the word is significant in the context of his conception of *Kāla* as *śakti* we shall be concentrating on the metaphysical import of the term *śakti*.

Before we have some detailed look at Bhartṛhari's use of the word *śakti* in the metaphysical context we must note that the word *śakti* may have two meanings – power as well as potentiality.[5] The One could transform itself into diversity if the One contains diversity as its potentiality. Since Bhartṛhari conceives *Śabdatattva-Brahman* as the Reality, *śakti* may to be understood in the sense of potentiality, as well as the power of transforming the potentiality of *Brahman*. While commenting on the *kārikā* Bhartṛhari elaborates:

> What is meant by "due to multiplicity of powers" is – Appearing as many, the powers which are mutually opposed and are identical with *Brahman*, accumulate in it which is essentially the Word. In a cognition in which many objects figure . . . such as earth, people, etc. do not affect the unity of cognition. There is no contradiction between the multiplicity of things like trees which are cognized and the unity of cognition. The form of the cognition does not really differ from that of the object because different forms of the object are not beyond the unity of cognition. Similarly, the powers which appear to be different from one another are not really so. . . . It appears to be different when it assumes the form of different objects which figure in it.[6]

We now find out that according to Bhartṛhari diversity is not opposed to unity as long as unity is seen as the potential womb of the diversity. Besides, by Oneness of *Brahman*, he means

---

5 The use of the word *śakti* with the double values occurs elsewhere in *Vākyapadīya*. For instance, Bhartṛhari deals with words or expressions having several meanings that are used as words with multiple potentialities:

ekasyāpi vivkṣāyām anunispadyate paraḥ ।
vinā bhisambhandhinā śabdaḥ śaktirūpaḥ prakāśate ।। – II.471

See Filiozat 2009: 216-17, 32.

6 *VP*, Vṛtti on I.2.

only the absence of differentiation and unity, not necessarily the number one.[7] This can help us to understand the logical link between *śakti* and *Śabdatattva-Brahman*. We must assume that the conception of *śakti* in no way stands in the way of the Oneness of *Śabdatattva-Brahman*. Therefore he conceives the first level of differentiation of *Brahman* by emphasizing on the multiplicity of potentialities (*śakti*). Yet Bhartṛhari insists that one must not thereby imagine that there is a dividing line between *Śabdatattva-Brahman* and its potentiality or power. For, in his *vṛtti* on *kārikā*, viz. I.4 Bhartṛhari clarifies:

> *ekasya sarvabījasya yasya ceyamanekadhā* ।
> *bhktṛbhoktāvyarūpeṇa bhogarūpeṇa ca sthitiḥ* ॥

> Of which One [*Śabdatattva-Brahman*] that is seed of all [*śabdabīja*], there is this state of multiplicity, that of the enjoyer, the enjoyed, and the enjoyment.

This One *Brahman* is the substratum of all powers which cannot be defined as identical or different from it. Again, in another context Bhartṛhari states:

> At any time, in any manner, everything in the phenomenal world exists as a bundle of power elements and hence has a variety of properties. Therefore it is intended to be conveyed as certain thing in a specific situation.[8]

> Both the *kārikās* state that a single entity, a substance is a conglomerate of multiple powers of which it brings about multiple effects. . . . As variety of expressions with reference to a single entity becomes possible in the world of everyday communication, so a variety of conceptualizations with reference to *Brahman* becomes possible through its powers.[9]

---

7 *VP*, Vṛtti on I.2.

8 *śaktimātrāsamūhasya viśvasyānekadharmaṇaḥ* ।
sarvadā sarvathā bhāvāt kvacid kiṁcid vivakṣyate ॥ – *VP*. III.7.2

9 Ogawa, Hideyo 2009: 245.

This indicates that the multiplicity of the powers of a substance (including *Brahman* that can be identified as the highest substance) does not affect the power of the substance. So we find that the manifestation of the power/potentiality is not different even though in the practical level it may appear as separate. In this context it is of interest to know that Vṛṣabha glosses the term *sarvabīja* in the *kārikā* I.4 quoted above as *bhinna śaktipracita*, "that which is filled with different *śakti* (powers)".

So it appears that the introduction of the notion of *śakti* is necessitated in order to secure self-identity of a single substance to which it is attributed and which has different kinds of potentialities to manifest. In the case of (*śakti*) power of *Brahman* Bhartṛhari identifies it as the *nimitta* (efficient cause) of the phenomenal world (*prakriyā jagato yataḥ*) and also as the seed of all (*sarvabīja*). But without assuming the unity between power and the wielder of power he could not have maintained his non-dualistic stand. This is the reason why while introducing the notion of power in his metaphysics he emphasizes on two different aspects – *apṛthaktva* (non-distinction) and *pṛthakatva* (distinction).[10] He has to maintain this distinction of the *Brahman* from its *śakti*s on the one hand and non-distinction from the *śakti*s on the other hand to relate the two levels – the transcendental level and the phenomenal level.

Kāla as Śakti

Finally introducing the notion of *Kāla* as a *śakti*, the third *kārikā* says:

> Depending on whose Time-power to which (though One) differentiation is attributed, the six transformations, birth, etc. become the cause of all variety in Being.

---

10 *apṛthakatve 'pi śaktibhyaḥ pṛthaktveneva vartate* । – *VP* I.2

With this *kārikā* Bhartṛhari elaborates how is the Undifferentiated Reality. *Śabda-Brahman* manifests itself as the diverse and ever-changing phenomenal world. It is already hinted in the first *kārikā* that he conceives the world as a process. And the process involves activity. From the above-mentioned *kārikā* it now becomes clear that it is *Kālaśakti* which stands for the principle of activity. Bhartṛhari defines an action as that which has parts arranged in sequence. So he defines *Kāla* as *nityakriyā* (eternal activity). From such presuppositions it now becomes clear that the phenomenal world is characterized by one unique feature, i.e. sequence. In the level of our thought and language the element of sequence figures very prominently. Our utterances are sequential. We cannot express all that we think or cognize simultaneously. In the level of utterance this feature is most predominantly displayed. Whenever we speak it has to be expressed syllable by syllable. By the time one syllable is uttered it is replaced by another. On the other hand, the world too is characterized by a continuous process that is sequential in nature. All animate and inanimate objects are liable to pass through the process of beginning, existence, growth and decay. So what is identified as object (*mūrti-vivartta*) is actually a series of sequential process (*kriyā-vivartta*). On the basis of such unique feature of the world and the word, Bhartṛhari formulates a metaphysical position wherein the world can be represented as a series of sequences. In other words, the world is not a totality of things/objects but a totality of events or states of affair. The events cannot be explained without reference to sequence and change. Thus both in the level of thought and in the level of the world of facts, sequence is the key element, that cannot be explained without reference to the phenomenon called Time (*Kāla*). But we must note that for Bhartṛhari the level of speech and the level of facts are not two unrelated phenomena.

The facts we experience in the empirical level are in any

case rooted in our speech potency, for our experience itself is word impregnated. The limit of our speech is the limit of our world. Thus without introducing the notion of time as the ground of the manifestation of the One and non-dual *Śabda-Brahman*, its transformation into the diverse and changeable world process would have remained unexplained. In fact, the very conception of temporal sequence holds clue to his conception of the phenomenal world. The notions of continuity and change that characterizes the empirical world can only be understood in terms of temporal sequence. The world consists of an infinite number of changing objects. Change means states and processes through which objects pass. According to Bhartṛhari all objects pass through at least three states, i.e. origin, continuity and destruction.[11] This presupposes temporal sequence. Again change presupposes objects that undergo change. Objects, on the other hand, are the products of previous processes and actions. Thus, the empirical world can be better understood in terms of temporal change. This may be the primary reason why Bhartṛhari conceives *Kāla* as that creative power (*svātantryaśakti*) of the *Brahman* due to which the non-sequential is manifested as sequential events and objects of the world. For, unless the notion of Time is brought in as one of the key concepts in explaining the relation between the Reality as the eternal and unchangeable principle, and the empirical world as characterized by change, the gap between the two appears to be unbridgeable.

The Dimensions of Kālaśakti

In the *vṛtti* of the third *kārikā* Bhartṛhari tries to explain the scope of the concept of *Kālaśakti*:

> All powers depending on their causes and having a starting point are governed by the creative power (*svātantrya*) called Time; they follow the modes of this time power. Because of

[11] *VP* III.9.3.

> the regulation of immense diversity of each object by means of prevention and permission, its appearances seem to have sequence. Time by allowing them to come to be, is the secondary cause of all transformations which depend on their own causes and also those whose production has been delayed. Its causal power being thus differentiated by manifestations which have a sequence, the differentiation which exists in the manifestations is attributed to it. It is like attributing to the balance by the divisions marked by the line on it at the time of balancing of the weight of the material which is in contact with it. *Thus sequence is attributed to something which is neither prior nor posterior in the form of "it was" or "it was not", the six transformations like birth, etc., become the source of modification of the changes in the Being.* – tr. K.A.S. Iyer

A close look at the *kārikā* as well as the *vṛtti* in a sense offers real clue to his metaphysics of Time. His position would be made gradually clear with the help of the *vṛtti* stated above.

Here the *Kāla* is not only presented as *śakti* of *Śabda-Brahman* but is posited as the primary ground of the transformation of the One and eternal Reality into the diversity and ever-changing phenomenal world. Bhartṛhari conceives Time to be the first power of *Śabdatattva* to enter into action in the process of transformation. Thus *Śabdatattva* may be seen as the womb of undifferentiated potentialities. *Kāla* is now presented as the initiator of six forms of transformations that is witnessed in the phenomenal world – birth, existence, change, growth, decay and destruction.[12] The above *vṛtti* also points to the

---

12 In this context we may get some clue from the grammatical theory of the *kriyā* (action) accomplished through six *kārakas*, like agent, object and instrument. The agent is all important here for it directs the action as per its will. The linguistic view here gets the ontological shade. Being is the fundamental action, the process of which there are six sub actions like birth and death. The agent is here *Śabdatattva*. Its nature of independence itself is *Kālaśakti*.

thesis that sequence, that is one of the basic features of the phenomenal world, is due to two fundamental activities of the *Kāla*, viz. suspension (*pratibandha*) and permission (*abhyanujñā*).[13] An activity or an object comes to being when time allows it to be manifested (*abhyanujñā)*, and it comes to an end due to the phenomenon called suspension (*pratibandha*). So the events of the world are characterized by a continuous process of beginning, sustenance and end. With the help of these two functions, *Kāla* initiates six forms of transformations.[14] Bhartṛhari says that *Kālaśakti* is only the locus (*upāśraya*) of this process of transformations. *Kāla* serves as the ground of transformation of the non-sequential into sequential, One into many, Unity into diversity. *Kāla* as *śakti* accounts for the diversity of the transformations and richness of the phenomenal world. *Kāla* as such is One and non-divisible, (*akhaṇḍa*) and non-changeable/non-sequential (*akrama*). Again, *Kāla* in the true sense of the term is timeless, for no units of duration can measure it. Thus it is inconceivable and inexpressible (*anirukta*). It is all-pervading (*vibhū*) as there is no difference between the *Brahman* and *Kāla* as its power.

Bhartṛhari, as is obvious from his commentary, ascribes independence (*svātantrya*) to *Kāla* as power. But *svātantrya* does not connote independence alone; it also signifies the creative power. Bhartṛhari calls it *kartṛśakti*. In his *vṛtti* he calls it *svātantrya*.[15] Helārāja interprets that *Kāla* as the *svātantrya śakti* in the sense of the "Power of Complete Freedom of *Brahman*".[16] According to him as the creative power, *Kāla* is responsible for

---

13 *VP* III.9.4.

14 These six forms of transformations are mentioned in the ancient text *Nirukta* I.2.

15 *kālākhyena svātantryena . . .* – *Vṛtti* on *VP* I.3

16 *Kālākhya svātntryaśaktirbrahmāni bhavādbhartṛhari abhiprāya*। – *Vṛtti* on III.9.1.8. Quoted from Iyer, Bhartṛhari, p. 338.

the birth, continuity and destruction of everything in the cosmos. Everything of course has its own special cause, material or other wise. But all these special causes depend on Time. Time is thus the auxiliary cause (*sahakārī kāraṇa*) of everything. Time is also compared to a wire-puller (*sūtradhāra*)[17] who pulls the wire of the machine (*lokayantra*), namely, the universe. It is due to time that there is sequence of things in the universe. Certain things appear at a particular time while other things do not appear at that time. Time controls their existence, puts them in sequence through the functions of *abhyanujñā* and *pratibandha*. But we should not confuse Bhartṛhari's simile of *sūtradhāra* with the theory of Time as destiny as advocated by the Kālavādins. They also delineate *Kāla* as the *sūtradhāra*, meaning thereby, destiny against which human beings are helpless puppets. But as is obvious from Bhartṛhari's explication of the *kārikā* he talks more about the process (sequentiality of the events) of the universe rather than the helplessness of man in the face of the invincible power of the *Kāla*. P.K. Majumdar rightly observes that Bhartṛhari's use of the word *lokayantra* rather reveals his scientific approach. Like a machine (*lokayantra*) the universe (including the human beings and the objects)[18] is guided by certain order and design. There is no scope for whim here. This order is due to the two functions of the *Kāla*. So Bhartṛhari's use of the word *sūtradhāra* should not drive us to the conclusion that he is following the philosophy of Kālavāda. His explication of the *jagat* as process implies actions and sequences in the phenomenal level. These sequences are due to two functions of *Kāla*, viz. *abhyanujñā* and *pratibandha*, as is evident from the 4th *kārikā* of the Kālasamuddeśa:

---

17 *tam-asya lokayantrasya sūtradhāram pracakṣyate* ।
pratibandhabhyanujñābhayām tena viśvam vibhājyate ॥ – III.9.4

18 Majumdar 2007: 3.

pratibandha abhyanujñābhām tena viśvam vibhajyate ।

It (time) divides the universe by *pratibandha* (suspension) and *abhyanujñā* (permission).

In this *kārikā* Bhartṛhari introduces two novel concepts – *abhyanujñā* and *pratibandha*. With these two concepts he explains the phenomenon called sequence that is the basic feature of the activities of the world. Thus *Kāla* is in no way identified with any form of determinism emphasized by the Kālavādin. If a thing is produced in the world it is because the Time allows power of its cause to be operative. Therefore certain things and events are produced at a particular time while the other events are produced at different point of time. This is due to *abhyanujñā*. Again *abhyanujñā* as a function of Time operates at two levels. It not only explains the origin of things but also their continuity. It is not enough that a thing must come to existence; it must continue to fulfil its purpose with the help of the accessories. When the object is no longer able to fulfil its purpose, it is destroyed due to the power of Time known as *pratibandha* (prevention). This function again has two aspects. It prevents the thing from coming into being before the proper time and also prevents them from continuing after the time. In its second aspect it is called *jarā* (old age). All the accessories that helped the object to fulfil its purpose desert it like ungrateful friends; and they lose their essential nature. Finally they perish. Thus, birth, continued existence and decay of objects are due to these two functions of Time.

Further elucidating the function of these two phenomena he says that all the objects are attached to the string of Time just as the small birds are used by the hunter as the baits to catch the bigger ones. These small birds are attached to the string and are allowed to fly or held back according to the wish of the hunter.[19] Similarly, objects and events are

[19] III.9.15.

manifested when their time comes, once manifested they continue to fulfil the purpose for which they are produced and once their purpose is fulfilled they perish.[20] So Time operates through two functions – either it allows a thing to be caused (*abhyanujñā*) or else it prevents the thing to be caused (*pratibandha*). But *Kāla* as such is without sequence, it is due to the eternal activity consisting of prevention and permission, the undifferentiated *Kāla* assumes differentiation and the form of sequence. So Bhartṛhari calls these two functions (*vṛtti*) as *śāsvatī* (eternal).[21] Operations of these two functions are fundamental to our understanding of why *Kāla* is called *svātantrya śakti*.

If we look at the metaphysical position of Bhartṛhari then we may notice that he has some conceptual obligation to introduce these two functions of *Kāla*. Without presupposing these two functions his initial thesis that world is another name for a process (*prakriyā*) would collapse. Whenever anybody is talking of process it implies change in the states of things that is not chaotic but harmonious. This is largely due to proper sequence of actions and events. So Bhartṛhari makes it clear:

> If Time did not suspend and did not remove the suspension, the states (of a being) would be confused, deprived of priority and posteriority.[22]

Elucidating the *kārikā* Helārāja says:

> In the absence of suspension affected by Time, the states (of being) would occur simultaneously; in the absence of the law of due sequence confusion of seed, sprout, stalk, stem, etc. would take place.

---

20 III.9.15.

21 III.9.30.

22 III.9.5.

If all the things and event would have appeared at the same point of time the edifice of causality would crumble. We would have a jumbled experience of the world. It is due to the march of Time the potentialities are realized. The potentialities are realized when urged by the Time. So Bhartṛhari ascribes the creative (*svātantrya*) power to *Kāla*.

Again Bhartṛhari designates *Kāla* as all-pervasive (*vibhū*), for all the states of the world process are permeated by the power of *Kāla* through the functions – *abhyanuñjā* and *pratibandha*. So Bhartṛhari conceives *Kāla* as the soul of the universe (*viśvātmā*), for "in every stage the operation of Time is established".[23]

> *pratyavastaṁ tu kālasya vyāpāra 'tra vyavasthitaḥ* ।
> *kāla eva hi viśvātma vyāpāra iti kathyate* ॥

> Here, i.e. in this world at every stage, the operation of time is established. So the activity called time is said to be the soul of the universe.

We note that in the above-mentioned *kārikā* Bhartṛhari uses the word *vyāpāra* (activity) to indicate why *Kāla* is to be taken as the soul or the essence of the universe. The activity that is associated with time is invariably connected with the process of sequence and change. Therefore highlighting on the dynamic aspect of the power called Time, he defines *Kāla* in a distinctly different way. He says:

> With motions similar to turnings and agitations of a water-wheel, (it is time) driving (*kālayati*) all parts (*kāla*, in the phenomenal sense) obtains the name *kāla*.[24]

Kāla does not serve as the passive background in the backdrop of which we place objects of the world. *Kāla* provides the necessary urge to events and objects so that they can be

---

23 III.9.12.

24 III.9.14.

manifested in the world process. It is conceived as the driving force.

Kāla and Creation

From the above discussion it clear that *Kāla* as a power is not to be confused with the cause and effect. The world is guided by the law of cause. But each cause is not due to time, but due to other circumstances. For example, when the seed is turned into the sprout, it is not the Time which directly helps the cause (seed) to turn into effect (sprout). The process would rather depend on such accessories as the nature of the soil, moisture, etc. But ultimately it is the Time that allows the effect to be produced when the right conditions are present. The power of Time is operative in all the states and events that exist at a particular point. Thus we find that Time is depicted as an efficient cause of the effect; for, other causes also have their role in the production of the effect. So we cannot explicate Time only in terms of cause–effect relation. The cause and Time together produce the effect. However, the power of permission/*abhyanujñā*, through which an object or event comes into being, and the power of prevention/*pratibandha*, when an object or event comes to an end, belong to Time. But in the scheme of Bhartṛhari's non-dualistic metaphysics there is no speculation or presumption about the manifestation of the world. So he discards both, the Satkāryavāda and the Asatkāryavāda. According to Satkāryavāda beginning is nothing but the manifestation of the unmanifested material cause; and the end is the merging of this in the unmanifested *prakṛti*. On the other hand, according to Asatkāryavāda beginning is a new creation, there is no potential cause involved (*prāgābhāva*); similarly end is total destruction (*dhvaṁśābhāva*). The former view is upheld by Sāṁkhya and the latter by Nyāya-Vaiśeṣika.[25] But Bhartṛhari argues:

---

[25] *VP* III, Kriyāsamuddeśa, 25.

> Just as, in some wonderful way, it is the sequenceless (*niṣkramam*), the causeless and the ineffable which is born, the same is true of its destruction.[26]

This *kārikā* reflects what he has already highlighted in 25th *kārikā* of Kriyāsamuddeśa and 38th *kārikā* of Jātisamuddeśa. These *kārikā*s make it clear that according to him the "Being" (*sattā*) has neither the beginning nor the end; hence *akramam* (non-sequential).[27] So the six transformations he talks about in relation to the empirical existence are only mentally constructed (*kalpita*). The entire viewpoint at first hand may seem complicated. It becomes more complicated because Bhartṛhari uses the word *adbhuta* (wonderful way) with reference to creation and destruction. But the use of this term actually does not mean anything mystical. Since he has again and again referred to the idea of *vivartta*,[28] for him the universe is an appearance of the One and sequenceless *Brahman*. In this format there is no scope of real transformation of one thing into another. So the world that we experience in time is due to the *vṛitti*s called *abhyanujñā* and *pratibandha*. Therefore, we presume that the world, characterized by sequence and creation, sustenance and destruction, is real. As everything that is a part of the sequential and differentiated world appears to be there so also it is destroyed without any cause. This is why the objects of the world pass through three transformations – creation, sustenance and the end. So *Kāla* is not directly related to any form of causality.

Bhartṛhari, following the general trend of the Indian culture, conceives Time as cyclic. But the empirical time is linear. The world undergoes the process of creation and dissolution

---

26 *yathaivādadbhūtayā vṛttyā niṣkramam ninirbandham* ı
apadaṁ jāyate sarvam tathāsyātmā prahiyate ıı – III.9.26

27 *VP*, Sambhandha Samuddeśa, 36.

28 VP 1.1; Jātisamuddeśa, 36.

(*pralaya*). At the end of the dissolution forces leading to next creation become manifest. As to how they manifest and where they become manifest, regarding such questions the philosophical positions differ. According Nyāya and Vaiśeṣika they manifest in the atoms (*paramāṇu*). According to Sāṁkhya they manifest in *pradhāna*. But according to Bhartṛhari Time signifies eternal action (*nityakriyā*). When the primitive urge to act becomes manifest it seeks through the universal, some substrata. It is not the object or substrata that undergoes change or sequence. Substrata itself is inexplicable. This substrata becomes distinct and identifiable when some universal quality inheres (*sahayoga*) in it. A being or substance by itself is neither this nor that, it is the association with the universal that it comes under a class name and then assumes an identity:

> Nothing is one or many, nothing is white or not-white. It is due to association with other things that substances appear this way or that way.[29]

It is due to its association with the quality that it is identified with an object. For example, when the quality of cowness inheres in the genus cow we call the object as cow. Similarly, when activities inhere in the objects we say that there is change, there is sequence or there is duration. Though the effects produced through particular causes are different, they are unified by the universal. So it is not the object which is prior or posterior, but the state of the being that changes from one state to another state is perceived as prior or posterior. As long as some universal is not associated with an object neither the concept time nor the causation is applicable. This is why universal is called the prompter (*prayojikā*)[30] of the causes and time is ascribed to activity.

---

[29] III.9.7.

[30] III.9.17.

Akhaṇḍakāla and Khaṇḍakāla

We have discussed how the primary intention of Bhartṛhari in hypothesizing Time as power is to explain sequence and action in the empirical world. At the same time I strongly feel that his ontological position regarding *Kāla* is best explicable if we keep his theory language in the backdrop. So let us have a re-look at some of the basic features of his theory of language. In the first canto of his *Vākyapadīya* Bhartṛhari has reiterated that no thought, no cognition, no experience is possible without the potentiality for linguistic expressibility. We express our experiences and thought about the phenomenal world in ordinary language. How do we go about it? We express our thought and communicate with one another in a sequential manner with the help of words and sentences, though they are intended to express a unitary sense (*sphoṭa*). It is the sequence (*krama*) in which our verbal expressions are made, but the sense/meaning expressed is unitary and non-sequential (*akrama*). One may take a clue from theory of language to understand how Bhartṛhari intends to present the principle of *Kāla* as One and unitary (*akhaṇḍa*). We may now presume that *Kāla* as a creative and unitary principle allows the human mind to arrange all their thoughts and experience in terms of the placement of events. Can the events, objects and actions be placed in right perspective without such notions as antecedent and consequent, sequence and simultaneity, fast or slow, prior or posterior, in terms of past, present and future? We talk of the duration of time and divide it in terms of units of time. We talk of such divisions as "moment", "hour", "day", "month", "year" and so on. Not only the experience of the outer world but our inner experiences are also placed in sequence. Such divisions facilitate our experience of the empirical world. Without such division the universe would be a static universe. So in our thought as well as in our discourse we talk not of Time but of "times".

But are we not landed in a paradoxical situation? How the One and unique principle of Time (*akhaṇḍakāla*) be understood only in terms divisible time (*khaṇḍakāla*)?[31] We have discussed in the previous chapter that as far as his philosophy of language is concerned he makes a conceptual distinction between *śabdatattva* (language as a principle) on the one hand, and *lokavyavahāra* (language in use) and *śāstra-vyavahāra* (language for analysis) on the other. The last two are characterized by division and sequences. In case of *lokavyavahāra* our language potency is manifested in multifarious forms (*vaikharī*). We may speak in different languages, in different forms of expressions. Therefore, diversity is its benchmark. But this verbal stage of the use of language refers to an inner stage which is called *madhyamā*. This is the pre-verbal mental stage (*madhyamā*), as our uttered speech is linked to the level of thought. But even in this stage of inner speech there is an implicit diversity. But ultimately all such diversities and division, both in the verbal level and pre-verbal level, lead to a deeper level called *paśyantī*. This is the non-verbal stage. The unity of the sense expressed lies here unmanifested. When the speaker intends to say something, he refers to this stage of unity (*paśyantī*) without which the unity of sense or meaning is not communicable. This is one of the reasons why Bhartṛhari advocates the theory of *akhaṇḍapakṣa* (as opposed to the prevalent theories like *abhihitānavaya* and *anvitābhidhāna*) that suggests that we always grasp the meaning of a sentence as a whole, though the words are presented one by one. The hearer does not keep on remembering the words and word-meanings syllable by syllable and mentally compute them to derive the sentence meaning from the individual words of a sentence. Again, if we look at language from the standpoint of Śāstra like grammar then also we take resort division. Texts are

---

31 Bhartṛhari often uses the word *kriyābheda* while discussing about the divisible time.

divided into sentences, words, letters, etc. We divide our utterances into parts of speech, into tenses, etc. But in the final analysis Bhartṛhari would say in uncertain terms that all such diversities and divisions in both levels, viz. *lokavyavahāra* and *śāstra-vyavahāra*, are artificial. They have use as long as the speaker and the hearer are communicating or we are analysing the language in terms of syntax or phonetics. They have practical use, but in principle, division does not reflect the true nature of the language as a principle (*śabda*). Divisibility ultimately points to the inherent non-divisibility of meaning (*sphoṭa*).[32]

This non-dualistic stance has its corresponding bearing in his ontological viewpoint too. Time as a principle stands for non-duality and indivisibility. At the same time the events and states of the empirical world are experienced in terms of duration, sequence, simultaneity, etc. But Time is different from various actions taking place in the cosmos. Rather these actions divide Time, which in fact is indivisible. Objects and their processes of growth, etc. may vary but that does not affect Time. It is like a road that is not affected by the passers by who travel on the road. Pedestrians and the traffic may stop but the road continues to be there. As Bhartṛhari says:

> The passing away of objects does not bring about the passing away of Time. The road is not affected by any difference in the movement of the people who walk on it.[33]

These diverse ways of presenting the events and actions of the world are, in the ultimate sense, unreal. Time is but One

---

32 As Helārāja points out, "... the soul of the manifested sound whose true nature is *sphoṭa*, which is same everywhere in the sphere of words and sentences, looks as if it were different, due to variations of sounds manifesting it" (III.9.66).

33 *VP* III.9.74.

but is imagined (*kalpate*) to be different with fixed limits.[34] According to Bhartṛhari, Time seems to be divided because of the divided alien activities (*dharmāntara*). For example, the movement of sun and planets are no part of Time,[35] yet it is due the movement of the sun or planets we add such appellation to it as time of origination, time of destruction, etc. So, when Time is perceived in conjunction with the alien activities it acquires such limitations (*upādhis*); and thus appears it to be divisible. Division is a superimposition; it is in no way integral to it. Bhartṛhari clarifies:

> . . . Time remaining (always) the same (becomes) within the sphere of normal usage, a moment, or world age (*manvantara*), because it is differently perceived by the intellect.[36]

As due to the movement of the sun we talk of day or night, month or year, similarly we use many other forms of events and processes that directly or indirectly refer to time divisions. It is the action that is measured as "slow" or "quick". Such notions as "prior", "posterior" and even "simultaneity" that indicate division of time are attributed to time are actually property of the events wrongly attributed to Time. We also talk of such divisions of time as seasons, such spring, summer, etc. as the manifestation of Time itself. But again this is a case of wrong attribution. It is like the same person being called a carpenter when he is chiselling the wood and blacksmith when he is hammering the iron;[37] or to take another example, a man is called a father when he is taking care of his child and an employee when he is at his workplace. Certain change in the environment helps us to label them as seasons. They are

---

34 III.9.8.

35 III.9.6.

36 *buddhyavagrahabhedāc ca vyavahārātmani sthiteḥ* ।
tāvān eva kṣaṇa kālo yugomanvantarāṇi vā ॥ – III.9.69

37 III.9.32.

determined by events and action. So time is the means of measuring such an immaterial thing as action.[38] In this context Bhartṛhari refers to a traditional method of measuring time consisting of a pot of water with a hole (water clock). The water in the vessel flows through the hole. The time taken by the vessel through the hole is a standard to measure time. The water passing through the hole is not Time, it is the amount of water which passes through the hole that helps us to measure the process.[39] Bhartṛhari says that the water passes in certain measure because of the two powers of Time, viz. suspension and permission. We may also take the example of an hour glass through which certain amount of sand passes depending on the size of the passage. Here we do not call the sand as time. Time as an entity is not measured. Since it makes the concept of measurement possible, Time as such is not measurable. Thus in the phenomenal world we comprehend everything in terms of time that is measurable and divisible. But it would be wrong to say that Time is divisible and measuarable.

I intend to discuss Bhartṛhari's notion of *khaṇḍakāla* in a separate chapter. We must remember that the conception of *khaṇḍakāla* is important for Bhartṛhari both as a linguistic non-dualist (Śabdādvaitin) as well as a philosopher of language. As a philosopher of language he would stick to the theory of the unity of the indivisible *sphoṭa*, yet he has to also admit the practical use of the diversity of the words. As a grammarian–philosopher he has the logical obligation to explain different forms of uses of the sentences that indicate the notion of time, including such notions as the use of tense (past, present and future) in our ordinary language. This equally applies to our use of words referring to time. No doubt, as a non-dualist he conceives Time as One. At the same time he admits:

---

38 *kālādevam kriyāgatiḥ* – III.9.28.

39 III.9.64; also 70-71.

> It is not possible for us to deal with the (world of things) without having recourse to time, which either exists as exterior one or as collection made by the intellect (as possessing powers dependent upon the intellect).[40]

For, we experience the events of the world that is exterior to us in sequence. Similarly, our thought that happens within too is sequential in nature. So in both the cases divisible time is presumed.

Despite the practicality of the notion of time-division (*khaṇḍakāla/kriyābheda*), Bhartṛhari would not grant any independent status (reality) to time divided in the ontological level. He very explicitly dismisses the reality of such concepts as existence, succession, sequence, that we believe to the very basis of our understanding of *khaṇḍakāla*. For example, as long as we are experiencing the worldly activities we take the concept of existence for granted. But he argues that a close look at the use of this concept reveals that our notions of existence and non-existence are associated with particularized time. For example, a thing is *not* before it comes into existence, *it is* when it has origination. Our mind however conceives the entire thing to be existent. So before its origination being non-existent an object has no succession, as the division into prior and posterior does not apply. When it is produced and existent, it too cannot be differentiated into prior and posterior as its nature persists. Having thus intelligently investigated (the matter), it can be conclusively said that there is no (i.e. can be no) reference to sequence (in the case) of both existing and non-existing beings. For sequence depends upon difference:

> Therefore, attributing of priority and posteriority (is done) by holding (considering) together (the two stages) in the mental level. These two modes are woven by the intellect

40 *jñānānugataśaktim vā bāhyam vā satyataḥ sthitam।*
kālātmānam anāśritya vyavahāratuṁ na śakyate॥ – III.9.58

> and are labelled as prior and posterior. There is first an idea of non-existent and then the idea of existent, the succession is otherwise an ideal. Similarly, sequence too is hypothetical.[41]

Thus *khaṇḍakāla* as such has no existence. It is presumed because it helps us to understand the phenomenal world in a systematic and coherent pattern. Yet a deeper look makes us realize that the very notion of *khaṇḍakāla* leads us to the point of non-differentiation and unity. We usually conceive of an eternal Time which makes it possible for the phenomenal activities to be restricted by temporal duration and succession. Time's division facilitates the separation of activities like beginning, end and sequence. This is the reason why Bhartṛhari calls the Time in the absolute sense as the instigator.

> For the restrictions concerning creation and manifestation are dependent upon this instigation. Because the existence (of the created objects) is dependent upon the conception of a single Time, existence follows the restrictions of Time.[42]

To sum up Bhartṛhari's position vis-à-vis *akhaṇḍakāla* (*Kālaśakti*) and *khaṇḍakāla* we may again refer back two angles that we notice in his analysis of the principle of Time. From the standpoint of philosophy of language it may be said that Time is never divided but our language functions in such a way that it appears that as if the Time itself is divided. It is not the Time which is actually changing. As long as we are dealing with the empirical world, cognizing it, experiencing it, expressing our ways of looking at it with ordinary language we believe that it is the time that is measured. So it is real. But ontologically speaking it is not actually touched by the events and objects; rather it is the objects or events which lead us to think of duration and time. Bhartṛhari compares the indivisible

41 Helārāja's Commentary on III.9.36.

42 *VP* III.9.10 (tr. P.S. Sharma).

Time with a weighing machine. The weighing machine gives the measurement of the object when it comes in contact with it. It is the paradigm of measurement that itself is immeasurable. We notice that objects are constantly changing, something is always being produced and something else is always perishing. This sequence which belongs to processes is attributed to Time. Sequence is primarily the property of action but it is attributed to something else.[43] In fact, Bhartṛhari would say that the notion of sequence itself is unreal. There is neither any sequence in the existing things nor in the non-existing things.[44]

However the entire notion of the reality of *akhaṇḍakāla* and unreality of the phenomenal time (*khaṇḍakāla*) needs to be delved deeper. Certain unresolved issues may still haunt us. For example, what is the exact relation between *khaṇḍakāla* and *akhaṇḍakāla*? What exactly is the status of the empirical world? Here the following *kārikā* and Helārāja's commentary might be helpful in throwing some light on the issue.

> It is the effect of Time that the appearance (*nirbhāsa*) of the universe, which in reality sequenceless, is perceived as if possessing sequence.[45]

Elucidating the *kārikā* Helārāja says:

> (A)s explained in the *Sambandhasamuddeśa* (3.3.81), the universe, (which is) an appearance of *Brahman* (the self-existent spirit), is devoid of sequence. (The fact) that this universe appears as having sequence is due to the ability of the suspension and permission effected by Time-power. For,

---

43 *VP* III.9.30 Helārāja's commentary.

44 *asataśca kramonāsti sahi bhettuṁ na śakyate* ।
satohapi cātmatattvaṁ yat tat tathaivāvasiṣṭhate ।। – III.9.36

45 *nitbhāsopagamo yohayaṁ kramavāniva dṛśyate* ।
akramasyāpi viśvasya tat kālasya viceṣṭitam ।। – III.9.46

the power of *Brahman* (which is called) Time (and which in reality is an appearance) bears fruits in individual souls, because it is the cause for the appearance of beings with sequence. This has already been decided in Brahma-kāṇḍa 1.3. This appearance which is equal to as if having sequence (is) indeed the first operation of Time here, i.e. universe.[46]

The above *kārikā* and the accompanying commentary make the following presuppositions clear:

1. The universe is an appearance (*vivartta*).
2. It is due to the principle called *Kālaśakti* that the non-sequential *Brahman* appears as the manifold activities of the universe characterized by sequence.
3. The sequence is due to *abhyanujñā* and *pratibandha*, the two basic functions of *Kālaśakti*.
4. *Kālaśakti* has its bearings upon the individual souls which itself is functional thorough sequential activities (that may include thought, speech and experience).
5. Finally, *Kālaśakti* is not real in the absolute sense. For, if *Kālaśakti* is Real then can we say that there is but one and Absolute Reality, viz. *Śabda-Brahman*?

Kāla and Avidyā

Bhartṛhari in accordance with his non-dualist position has to dismiss the Reality of all other principles except *Śabda-Brahman*. So, the question arises, why did then he talk of *Kālaśakti* as the creative power of the *Brahman*?

Bhartṛhari to maintain non-dualistic ontological stance introduces the concept of *avidyā* (III.9.62) to offer a satisfactory answer to the issue. He proclaims:

prathamaṁ tadavidyāyāṁ yad vidyāyām na vidyate

---

46 Trs. P.S. Sharma 1972.

> That (the conception of Time) is the first stage of *avidyā* which is not there once the right knowledge (*vidyā*) dawns.

It now seems clear that Bhartṛhari finally dismisses the very concept of the eternal *Kāla*, for it has no status once true knowledge about the Reality is realized. It is now obvious that *avidyā* is the root of our conception of *Kālaśakti*. But one may very validly ask – why is it presumed first of all? The answer is simple. No philosopher can discard the existence of the empirical world, whether it is conceived as appearance or as reality. Philosopher, in any case, has to start with the worldly experience that is characterized by change and diversity. Depending on the ontological predilection some would move from diversity to unity, from change to unchanging principles; while some others would prefer to explain the world in terms of diversity and change. As is well-known Bhartṛhari is one of the first thinkers who offered a systematic account of non-dualistic metaphysics (Advaita-vāda). So he has the logical compulsion to introduce the concept of *avidyā* to relate the One and unique *Brahman* to the empirical world. This is the reason why in the commentary on the very introductory verse of *Vākyapadīya*, he explicitly states:

> It is solemnly declared that *Brahman* is beyond all representations; it is endowed with all powers which are neither identical with it nor different from it; it has two aspects, that of unity (*vidyā*) and that of diversity (*avidyā*), (even in the aspect of *avidyā*), it is really free from diversity; it is in all states, unaffected by beginning and end, even though manifestations appear in worldly transactions in a spatial and temporal sequence.[47]

So according to Bhartṛhari, the apparent knowledge and experience of the diversity is another name for *avidyā*.

---

[47] Tr. Iyer.

Elaborating further the two key concepts, viz. *avidyā* and *Kālaśakti*, Helārāja comments:

> This then is the conception of time. Within nescience (*avidyā*) which is the cause of the phenomenal world, there emerges first of all the phenomenal world (*saṁsāra*), consisting in the appearance of differentiation. Differentiation is spatial and temporal. Of the two the temporal difference comes first in the creation of the world.[48]

In Kālasamuddeśa he sticks to his original position. He holds that the undifferentiated Ultimate Reality (*avikalpa*) becomes differentiated and assumes infinite number of forms. Helārāja explains that this is due to *avidyā* coming down from eternity. The universe which is manifested under its influence consists, first of all, an infinite number of experiencers (*bhoktā*s) who are really identical with the Ultimate Reality, being essentially of the nature of consciousness. But they appear to be different from it and also different from one another because of *avidyā*. They experience the universe which, like their own consciousness, is also an emanation from the *Śabdatattva-Brahman*.

This is clear from the above remark that Bhartṛhari holds that it is the individual self, the enjoyer (which is of the nature of consciousness), who under the influence of *avidyā* conceives the universe (both beings and non-beings) as differentiated. For, *avidyā* (ignorance) holds no meaning without the conscious human beings as its locus. It is ignorance which conceals the true nature of *Brahman* as well as *ātman*, for, they are non-different. In case of individual self

> consciousness in the form of *paśyantī* is without sequence, but when it is associated with *prāṇa* principle (activity), it shines as Time, as though it had sequence. . . . The reality

48 *ataḥ evaitat kāladarśanam*, as tr. Iyer 1969: 123.

> called *Brahman* is without any sequence and consists of true knowledge and it is not affected by Time. Under the influence of nescience (*avidyā*), it assumes sequence and appears as this or that. *Thus through the intervention of Time, the phenomena appear in temporal sequence to the individual selves, coming down from the time immemorial.* All differentiations consist of nescience. All divisions of Time adopted from different points of view are also the creations of *avidyā*. Again, once true knowledge dawns all differentiation disappears, and therefore division (of time) also disappears. Therefore, to discuss whether it (the division is right or not, would result in labour only). In the empirical stage, everything is unreal and the truth cannot be determined. This is the substance of what is meant.[49]

To understand Bhartṛhari's position we have to go back to the basic presuppositions of his metaphysics. He is taking a unique position on the concept of Time from the standpoint of a philosopher of language. Time is there because consciousness is there. It is the man who looks at the world from the prism of Time. Had there been no consciousness, no languaging being, there would be no use of the concept of time. He has stated very categorically that human consciousness is intertwined with word-consciousness. For, a man as a conscious being experiences the world through concepts; and concepts are language-determined. So a man experiences phenomena of the world, including his own existence in time. Again, on the other side of the scale stands a man with the right knowledge (*vidyā*). He realizes that he is but non-different from *Brahman*, once he gets rid of his *avidyā* and obtains *vidyā* neither the Time exists for him, nor the divisions of time. Here we come across a pure non-dualistic (*advaita*) metaphysical position.

---

[49] Iyer 1969: 123.

The way the concepts *avidyā* and *Kālaśakti* have been dealt within Bhartṛhari's philosophy may tempt the scholars to compare note with another great non-dualist – Śaṅkarācārya. It is no doubt a fact that both Śaṅkara and Bhartṛhari subscribe to a theory of Advaita. But it must be kept in mind that Bhartṛhari is offering a non-dualistic metaphysics from the standpoint of a philosopher of language. Śaṅkarācārya, on the other hand, is handling his non-dualism from the standpoint of pure metaphysics. There are certain concepts in Bhartṛhari's philosophy, viz. *Kālaśakti* and *avidyā*, which may be compared to Śaṅkara's notion of *māyā* and *avidyā*. However, such comparisons can be fruitful if we go into the details of these fundamental concepts. So I have planned to discuss these concepts in a separate chapter.

Both, *avidyā* and *Kālaśakti* play a crucial role in salvaging the basic non-dualism of Bhartṛhari. As Helārāja points out, the former (*avidyā*) brings about differentiation in the undifferentiated and the later (*Kālaśakti*) is responsible for the temporal sequence in which the differentiated phenomena are presented to the individual perceiver. Once somebody looks at the world as projected by Time, world is for him is not a conglomeration of objects but a series of infinite number of changing objects. Change means states and processes through which an object passes. But this way of looking at the world through the lens of Time does not strike a discordant note as far as his stand as a philosopher of language is concerned. He had already made his stand clear by proclaiming – *kiṁ asmākam vastugatena vicareṇa*? (deliberation on the nature of the world of objects is of what use to us?)

4

Time as a Substance
Nyāya-Vaiśeṣika

NYĀYA and Vaiśeṣika systems are perhaps the only schools of Classical Indian philosophy that accord the status of reality to *Kāla*. In all probability much before Bhartṛhari composed his *Vākyapadīya* the idea of Time as an eternal and all-pervading principle was quite explicitly advocated by the Vaiśeṣikas. This may be one of the reasons why Bhartṛhari opens his discussion on the notion of Time in Kālasamuddeśa by placing the Vaiśeṣika view on the issue. As I have stated earlier, Bhartṛhari never presented the views of the other schools of thought as *pratipakṣa*. He simply states other's views, sometimes agreeing with them, sometimes refuting them without the arrogance of a dialectician. In the first *kārikā* of the Kālasamuddeśa he writes:

> Some have declared Time to be a substance (*dravya*), one, different from action, eternal, all-pervasive, which measures things in action.

Helārāja's commentary on this *kārikā* reads as follows:

> According to Vaiśeṣikas, time is said to have as its characteristic sign . . . the relation "prior, posterior", etc. (*Vaiśeṣika-Sūtra* II.2.6); it is all-pervading, SINGLE, formless and for this very reason it is not produced, eternal, different from activity, the dividing factor of things by means of activity such as creation etc. . . .[1]

[1] Tr. Sharma.

The *kārikā* as well as the commentary perhaps provides the finest gist of the Vaiśeṣika account of Time. We have noted in the previous chapter that Patañjali also delineates *Kāla* in a similar line. However, it may appear quite astonishing that such diversely distinct metaphysical systems like Nyāya-Vaiśeṣika, on the one hand, and Bhartṛhari on the other hand, opt to stand on the same platform so far as the notion of Time is concerned. Nyāya and Vaiśeṣika share a realistic and pluralistic ontology as opposed to Bhartṛhari's non-dualistic and idealistic metaphysical stance. Yet they conceive *Kāla* as One, eternal and all-pervasive. Both the sides stick to the postulate that eternal Time is timeless and the empirical events are temporally measurable. Both the sides agree that the notion of measurable time is associated with action. But for Nyāya-Vaiśeṣika, Time is a substance; not the only substance, but one out of nine substances like earth, water, air, fire, ether and mind. These substances are real in the sense that they make the experience as well as the existence of the empirical world possible. Bhartṛhari, on the other hand, does not offer the status of reality to the empirical world. It is just a projection of the One and undifferentiated *Śabda-Brahman*. But he elevates the conception of *Kāla* to a supreme position by labelling it as the power/potentiality of the Reality Supreme. In course of our discussion of the Nyāya-Vaiśeṣika theory of *Kāla* as *dravya*, the commonalities and disparities between both the stands will be made clear.

Time is defined in Nyāya-Vaiśeṣika either as the cause of our use of temporal expressions or of our knowledge of priority, posteriority, simultaneity or non-simultaneity, sooner or later, etc.[2] So we note that there are two angles from which the problem of time has been discussed – from the standpoint of the linguistic usage and from the standpoint of ontology.

2 *Bhāṣya* of Praśastapāda, quoted in Keith 1992: 457.

Both the angles cannot be independently presented for the ultimate concern for the philosopher is to systematize the facts in our thought and words. Philosophers cannot afford to ignore certain common concepts, including the concept of Time. Unlike the scientists they do not have facts at their disposal. They have mostly relied on human usages as their tool, as has been pointed out by Bhartṛhari. Such usages provide clue to our explanation about the key concepts that help one to have better assessment of the universe that he talks about, thinks about and experiences. So semantics and language analysis (*śabda-pramāṇa*) has all along been a part the Indian philosophical tradition (whether independent status is offered to it or not). In Nyāya-Vaiśeṣika too, we notice that it connects the two angles while elucidating the concept of Time. Despite this basic commonality between the two angles of dealing with the problem of Time I would like to address them separately, viz. ontological and linguistic. Nyāya-Vaiśeṣika, especially Nyāya school of thought, provides some in-depth and sophisticated analysis of this issue, that includes such problems as (i) is time a matter of perception?, and (ii) are the inferences about the existence of Time are foolproof? Besides we come across distinctly differing opinions, especially formulated by the later Naiyāyikas. However though interesting, I cannot go into such details of the arguments and counter-arguments as my focus in this work is on Bhartṛhari's conception of Time. So what follows is more or less a broad-based analysis that would be relevant for our purpose.

Kāla as a Dravya

In the earlier works of Vaiśeṣika the need of presuming time as an independent substance has been necessitated to explain certain common notions of temporal measurement. As Vaiśeṣika advances a form of atomistic pluralism that is mainly structured on a group of categories (*padārtha*) there is some metaphysical obligation on their part to discuss the notion of time. *Padārtha* literally means "the meaning of a word" or "the object signified by the word". *Padārtha* therefore implies an object that can be thought (*jñeya*) and named (*abhidheya*). Yet being realists they cannot conceive *padārthas* as categories of knowability alone but as that which categorizes all knowable objects that are real. *Dravya* (substance) is one of the seven categories along with such *padārthas* as *guṇa* (quality), *karma* (action), *sāmānya* (universality) and *viśeṣa* (particularity). They are real in the sense that all knowledge points to an object beyond and independent of it.[3] *Dravya*, one of the primary *padārthas*, is defined as the substratum where *karmas* and *guṇas* inhere; and which is the coexistent material cause of the composite entities produced from it.[4] Like all other *padārthas* *dravya* is real. But all nine of them do not possess the same characteristics. Some of them are atomic, plural and infinitesimal, such as earth and water. But space and time are conceived as eternal, indivisible, one and all-pervading. These two substances provide as if the canvas in which objects and events are placed. In this sense both space and time provide immense conceptual support to the realistic Vaiśeṣika ontology.

The Ontological Angle

From the above discussion it is clear that Nyāya-Vaiśeṣika accepts time as an independent category of reality. Since they take *Kāla* as eternal, they definitely refer to a different sort of concept that is distinct from our ordinary usage of time-words. It obviously refers to the *kāla* with capital K, i.e. *Kāla*. In its eternal aspect this is also called *mahākāla*. So according to Nyāya-Vaiśeṣika Time has following characteristics as a category of existence (*padārtha*). As an object or event cannot be conceived without Time as its background, it is eternal

---

3 *na caviṣaya kacid upalabdhiḥ* – *Vaiśeṣika Sūtra* I.1.15.

4 *kriyāguṇavat samavāyī kāraṇam dravyam* – ibid.

(*nitya*), beginningless (*anādi*) and endless (*ananta*). Moreover, as Time is non-composite (*nirāṁśa*) and does not depend on any other substance as its locus it is independent (*svatantra*), and also the receptacle of all that is contingent (*ādhāra*). Time is further characterized as all-pervading (*vibhū*), as it is in contact with all that is finite.[5] The all-pervasive substances are never contained in anything (*ādheya*). It has no form (*amūrtta*). Time is uniform and ubiquitous. It has no parts (*niravayava*). It is inherently unitary (*eka*) and indivisible (*avibhājya*). As no change in terms of action or modification is conceivable without Time as its necessary frame of reference, it is itself inactive or unchanging (*niṣkriya*). The argument is that time, being a necessary condition for all movement and change, must itself be free from these attributes.[6]

But the question may arise – how do we know that such an eternal and indivisible *mahākāla* exists, as it not subject to direct perception? Nyāya-Vaiśeṣika provides logical grounds for such a conception of Time. According to them the knowledge of Time is arrived at by a series of inferences. The position can be said to be totally in conformity of Nyāya position since Nyāya-Vaiśeṣika accepts inference as the valid means of knowledge (*pramāṇa*).

First, the notions of priority (*paratva*) and posteriority (*aparatva*) of simultaneity (*yaugapadya*) and succession (*ayaugapadya*), and of quickness (*kṣipratva*) and slowness (*ciratva*) constitute the grounds (*liṅga*) of inference of the existence of Time. We look at the world and often describe the happenings of the world through such time-concepts. But what is the basis of such usages? The Vaiśeṣika thinkers like Vācaspati Miśra and Udayana provide some cogent argument

---

5 *sarvamūrtasaṁyoganuyogitva* – *Bhāṣā Pariccheda* 22.

6 The above discussion is based on Śrīdhara's *Nyāyakandalī* 19 as well as Śaṅkara Miśra's *Upaskāra* 17 where detailed enumeration of the ontological properties of time is found.

in favour of their theories. According to them relation among the objects such as prior and posterior is usually believed to be grasped through solar motion (*ādityagatiparivartanī*). But solar motion is not directly connected with the objects. So Time is inferred as the via-media. Their analysis is as follows: when an object is taken as prior in relation to one and posterior to another, what can serve as the basis for the attribution of such qualities to a given object? It may be argued that the former is connected with a larger number of solar revolutions than the latter. But there can be a direct relation of inherence only between the sun and solar motion but not between the object in question and the sun, which are remotely separated from one another. Again the movement of the sun inheres in the sun alone. So there is no relation of inherence (*samavāya*) between the sun and the object. This presupposes that there must something else that makes the contact possible. To have the necessary contact the category has to be all-pervading. None of the all-pervading categories like *ākāśa* (ether), *ātman* and *manas* can act as the connecting link between the solar motion and the objects. Thus, there has to be a common medium which can serve as a link between the two, and which, moreover, is capable of transmitting the quality of one to the other. Through the application of the method of exclusion it is argued that no other substance can perform this specific function; thus, leading to the inference of an all-pervading Time.

The above argument may prove that *Kāla* is all-pervading, but on what grounds we can call it as eternal? Nyāya-Vaiśeṣika takes the notion of causality to prove their point. If the things of the world are real, then they must have been caused; for, no production or destruction of any object that is a part of the world could be explained without being connected with the notion of cause. The Nyāya and Vaiśeṣika philosophical literatures contain detailed discussions on the problem of causality and its implications. From the detailed discussion and debate they carry out on this issue it becomes clear that their theory of causality discloses a conceptual structure, where the question of Time is of vital importance. They offer some valid arguments which lead to the formulation of the idea of absolute time as a necessary presupposition for causal operation. According Nyāya-Vaiśeṣika the universe consisting of the "reals" is to be classified into two: those which are subject to production and destruction (the non-eternal), and those which are not so (the eternal). An eternal entity like *ākāśa* is uncausable because it is never non-existent, which means that it is timelessly existent. An absolute non-entity like a square circle is equally uncausable because it is ever non-existent, which means that it is timelessly non-existent. Causation, therefore, is possible only in the case of an event which is contingent (*kadācitaka*), i.e. which comes into being after having been previously non-existent. In other words, previous non-existence, which is intelligible only in the sense of a temporally determined non-existence, transpires to be the necessary condition of the production of an event. If, therefore, there were no time, there could be no happening, and things would either merely exist or not exist at all. Causality, thus, is found to be inexplicable without reference to Time.

Cause is defined as that which is a necessary and invariable antecedent to an event.[7] Here, the idea of antecedence has an immediate temporal reference. The effect succeeds the cause, which evidently involves the idea of time. But it should be remembered that temporal antecedence is not the only mark of the cause. It is the sum total of all the necessary causal antecedent factors (*sāmagrī*). The production of the effect is its first conjunction with time. The causal operation does not

[7] *ananyathāsiddhaniyataourvabhāvitam kāraṇatvam* – *Tarkabhāṣā* of Kesava Mishra 25.

consist of merely manifesting the potentially existent, as the Sāṁkhya claims, but of creation of what was non-existent. So the occurrence of the effect is an event-in-time. So the causal operation, i.e. the production of the effect in Time, leads one to admit that the idea of Time as an ontological reality.[8] Even the very definition of cause is possible only on the premise of the ontological reality of Time, with reference to which the idea of sequence of the cause and the effect can be meaningfully understood.

Udayanācārya[9] provides some of the basic arguments in his *Nyāyakusumāñjali* to prove why the concept of causality is so fundamental to our understanding of the processes of the world. He argues, if an event is to be taken as uncaused, it could happen at any time or all the time. The fact that is happens only at a determinate time and not otherwise indicates that there is an antecedent cause for its production. Therefore coming into being of all that is contingent can be explained only on the basis of the assumption of a cause. Since Nyāya does not accept the pre-existence of the cause (Satkāryavāda) as propounded by Sāṁkhya, the very notion of cause signifies the cessation of the prior non-existence of the effect. Besides, no event can be said to produce itself. Its occurrence is determined by the cause, which is temporally antecedent. Moreover, an event or an entity cannot come out of nothing. If this could be admitted then an event could happen just about any time or at any place. So we have to presume the conceptual validity of the notion of cause. But at the same time Udayanācārya makes it clear that the idea of cause is applicable only in connection with that whose existence is qualified by a previous non-existence. This prior non-existence is obviously a temporal reference, pointing to the

---

8 *Vaiśeṣika Sūtra* 2.2.11(17) *kāraṇe kālākhyā.*

9 Udayana, *Nyāya Kusumāñjali* 1.4-5 and the prose commentaries thereon.

fact that all causal operation is necessarily an event in Time. Therefore we cannot conceive of an event without Time being taken as its receptacle (*ādhāra*). Denying the status of an objective reality of *Kāla* is as good as presenting a static universe, which would be without any change or movement. As Time (as an indivisible and single principle) is indispensable for all that happens in the world characterized by events that are contingent by nature, Time is conceived as the instrumental cause of the contingent objects.[10]

However, the concept of contingency and the concept of causality are interdependent. Without the idea of causal operation, entities would be taken as either as ever-existent or never-existent. If we accept causal operation as a case of Asatkāryavāda then it is automatically implied that Time is the very basis of the activities of the world. The contingent process of coming into being and going out of being is possible in the background of an eternal and singular entity called Time.

The notion of Time is also derived from our experience of change. Material bodies, whether inorganic or organic, are found to pass through successive states and modifications. And this can be explained only on the supposition that it is time that makes a difference to the bodies and helps their development or decay. When an old man is seen to possess physical peculiarities different from those of his young son, the contrast inevitably points to a difference in physical change, and time is inferred as the cause of it. In all such cases, the changing substances are supposed to be in direct connection with time, for, on no other hypothesis can change be explained.

Again, Time is essential to all the changes in nature such as production, destruction and sustenance. It is not the cosmic power that causes the movements but is the condition of all movements. All things are perceived as changing and moving.

10 Cf. *janyam janakaḥ kālaḥ* – *Bhāṣā-Pariccheda* of Viśvanātha 22, 45.

But the objects do not have the power of self-generation and self-movement. If that would have been the case there would not be mutual relation of things that persists in spite of all changes. All movements in the world is ordered which implies that there has to be reality which is in general relation to all changes. Time is regarded as the independent, real, pervading the whole universe and making the ordered movement of all things possible. Thus the realistic metaphysical scheme of Nyāya-Vaiśeṣika encompasses the reality of Time or *Kāla*. So Time cannot be taken as merely a subjective construction (*buddhi-nirmāṇa*).

Now let us go back to the question of Time as the unitary principle. The philosophers of these schools point out that all the marks or grounds (*liṅga*), which serve as basis for inferring Time, point to it as one. The manyness of time, i.e. the conventional time divisions, can be explained with the help of limiting adjuncts such as the solar motion, etc. on the basis of the postulation of a singular, ubiquitous time. There are the actions denoting past, present and future. These do not imply any inherent division or plurality in the Time as such.

Before we wind up our discussion on this section it should be kept in mind like Bhartṛhari that Nyāya-Vaiśeṣika admits two dimensions of *Kāla* – the eternal, indivisible Time (*akhaṇḍakāla*) and the Time-divided (*khaṇḍakāla*), i.e. time as duration in terms of day, month, moment, earlier, later, etc. This topic will be taken up in a separate chapter.

The Linguistic Angle

I have stated in the beginning of this chapter that Nyāya-Vaiśeṣika defines Time *either as the cause of our use of temporal expressions* or of our knowledge of priority, posteriority, simultaneity or non-simultaneity, sooner or later, etc. Thus far I have been concentrating on the ontological issue that leads the Nyāya-Vaiśeṣika philosophers to logically establish the knowledge of the reality of *Kāla*. Let us now examine how they handle the issue from a linguistic angle. Once the eternality and all-pervasiveness of Time are admitted we have to acknowledge that "Time" does not signify the measurable time that is expressed by such statements of the ordinary language like "the time of birth" or "the time of the commencement of an activity". Our ordinary language is replete with such usages that refer to time in our day-to-day conversation. All such usages are about the temporal measurement. Yet *Kāla* obviously refers to a principle beyond the ordinary temporal measurement. For the word *Kāla* does not mean the measurement that the ordinary usages such as "past", "present", "future", "month", "year" or "moments" do. So the distinction between the Time as such and the measurable time is already admitted by both the Vaiśeṣika and the Nyāya schools of thought.

From their account it is clear that the word *kāla* that stands for the eternal and indivisible principle; and does not mean temporal measure. So Time and time-words are distinct. Time-words imply units of measurement that could be determined by such factors as the rotation of the sun or planets. They, in other words, refer to units. At the same time, Naiyāyikas find good reasons for using the word "time" in two senses, viz. indivisible and divisible. "What unites the two senses is that the word time signifies a certain magnitude in that it primarily signifies what has magnitude."[11] Like spatial magnitudes or extension, temporal magnitude also characterizes things. As per Vaiśeṣika metaphysics magnitude (*parimāṇa*) is one of the twenty-four types of qualities that inhere in some substance. Any substance, that stands in conjunction with every substance in the universe has motion, has infinite magnitude. So whenever we use any word signifying temporal duration we

---

[11] Mukhopadhyaya 2009: 66.

must refer to *Kāla* or Time, which has infinite magnitude. But there is a clear-cut distinction between duration and magnitude. Time itself is not a temporal duration. For by the words "infinite magnitude of time" we do not mean infinite duration. Its infinity is not measurable quantity involving addition of infinite units of durational time. In this sense *Kāla* is ubiquitous. So this ubiquitous time is indivisible, without parts. But time has another use also, i.e. "time-words" like prior and posterior.

Again, there is another sort of temporal magnitude that comes to surface in our use of the words representing the verb words in language. The use of tenses in the verb shows that there are periods of time like past, present and future. Such verb-words refer to actions or occurrences of events. They are impermanent, relative and measurable units or sum of units of time. Nyāya tries to provide an account of such divisions of time in terms of the movement of the sun (*ādityagati*). Presumption of two types of time helps the Naiyāyikas to avoid the usual charge that one who admits measurable time and distinctions of past, present, future places himself under the compulsion of admitting infinite number of times, i.e. getting involved in infinite regress. Eternity of one Time is based on the postulate that it is a substance and it has no parts. Anything that is a substance and is indivisible can have no beginning and no destruction. Whether such substances actually exist is not important but our usages and incontrovertible experience of such usages prove that we can talk of such a substance meaningfully. Our usages involving time-words reveal that the word Time does not really mean magnitude whereas other time-words like days and months do. As one of the nine *dravyas*, Time is an item of reality. Yet, Time cannot be used to measure relative temporal duration of an event. The reason why time cannot be used to measure for measuring duration is that it is unlimited. Only things having limitation can be measured. We use such time-words like days or months to measure relative span of life in things as they have limited dimension. Measuring time means measuring events in time. We measure events by using units of measurement. We use such units of measurement as a day, a month, a moment, etc. But they have a limit. Even the largest span of duration we measure by this process is still limited, as the largest unit can be used to measure the relative unit of events. But Time does not exist in any of such units of measurement. A day, for example, is a certain section of the movement of the sun. But it still is a measurable time. So all types of units of measurement be it a moment, or a day or month are called time in a derivative sense of being measure of time.

> Our usages about different times or periods of time force us to admit that one Time is used *as different* times (actually, periods of Time artificially created by convention) when taken as qualified by or related to different things. For example, one single space is referred to as different spaces – space covered by this room or that room. Actually the rooms are different not the space. Space is used as only different when taken in relation to different sets of walls that enclose space. Similarly time is only used as different when taken in relation to such limited things as action or motion that has a beginning or end.[12]

In this context one may very validly ask – if we can measure time in terms of days or months why posit an extra entity called Time? In reply Nyāya-Vaiśeṣika philosophers argue that without admitting it we cannot make sense of that part of our usages, which involve reference to relative duration of events in Time. Definitely a philosopher does not need facts to prove his point. He has at his disposal certain concepts and their usage.

---

12 Mukhopadhyaya 2009: 66.

There is another explanation for the presumption of an eternal and indivisible Time. We may call it causal explanation. We talk about the facts of the empirical world in terms of earlier, later, sequence, simultaneity, etc. We cannot explain such usages in terms of the motion of the sun. So we have to admit that Time as a principle is one of the causes of *such usage*. For, the sun does not have direct contact with the events that we use in the sense of earlier or later. But both movement of the sun and duration of the event that is measured are in Time. So through Time the necessary relation is established between them, without which there could not have been a relation of cause and effect between them; and we could not have established such usages.

Thus on the basis of how we use our language Nyāya-Vaiśeṣikas admits two sorts of time – one real, uncreated, and eternal Time; and the other that has a beginning and end, in other words, a limited time. The former is eternal either in the sense of time transcending or in the sense of everlasting in time. The latter is said to be in time as it does not share the qualities of Time as *dravya*. So the durational and divisible time is often known as *kalpita* or *kriyopalakṣita* (imaginary) time. Such durational time is created and is measurable due to linguistic conventions created by us.

Our discussion on the Nyāya-Vaiśeṣika notion would not be complete if do not point out certain change of standpoint that occurred in the later phases of its development. Raghunatha Siromani, a reputed philosopher of the Neo-Nyāya (Navya-Nyāya) school, questioned the traditional view of absolute Time. In his work *Padārthatattvanirūpaṇam* he challenged the entire categorical framework that was current in the old Nyāya-Vaiśeṣika pluralistic, metaphysics. He criticized the plural categories of existence and questioned their validity. It is in this connection he also scrutinized the traditional understanding of time and space. The Nyāya-

Vaiśeṣika not only accepted the uniqueness and ubiquitousness of time on the basis of its ontology but on the basis of the judgement that we make in day-to-day life referring to sequence of events. The old school of Nyāya justified that division of (*khaṇḍakāla*) on the basis of the presupposition of the universal, indivisible, all-pervasive time (*mahākāla*) is conceived as limited by qualifying adjuncts (*upādhi*). He argues that although the variety of judgements dependent on qualifying adjuncts limiting an all-pervading substance like Time, it continues to remain the same. So in order to maintain the eternality and all-pervasiveness of space and time Raghunatha Siromani argued in favour of identification of Space and Time with God, which is conceived as an all-pervading substance. But at the same time while dismissing the independence of Time as a substance he proposed a new category called moment (*kṣaṇa*). However, this amendment of Raghunatha Siromani to abandon the conception Time as an independent substance was not approved by the later adherents of the school. They argued that the idea of one, all-pervading substance called Time as an independent *dravya* cannot be dropped without disturbing the logic of the metaphysical pluralism. Without admitting the notion of Time as a substance, many of the indigenous theses, right from the doctrine of creation to the notion of objects and their order in the universe, would collapse.

Nyāya-Vaiśeṣika vis-à-vis Bhartṛhari

From our brief discussion about Nyāya-Vaiśeṣika conception of Time as a substance we discover that these two allied systems of thought present a distinctive view of time that perhaps has no parallel in the Brāhmanical tradition (six approved orthodox schools of classical Indian philosophy). Even we do not come across a similar view in the non-orthodox tradition like Jainism and Buddhism. In this respect Nyāya-Vaiśeṣika radically differ from the Sāṁkhya, Yoga though they share a realistic metaphysics. In the previous chapter we have discussed Bhartṛhari's metaphysical system that is based on pure non-dualism of Śabdādvaitavāda. Yet the concept of *Kāla* as key principle does not in any way disturb its original Advaitic position. In contrast, we have now at our hand a metaphysical scheme that is radically opposed to non-dualism, as it stands by a realistic pluralism. Yet it not only admits the reality of *Kāla* but also presents it as One, eternal, all-pervading independent reality. The way the concept of *Kāla* is handled by Nyāya-Vaiśeṣika one notices strange similarities between them and Bhartṛhari. Both the sides entertain same conceptual format including the idea of the indivisible Time as distinct from the measurable time. Interestingly, both the systems of thought look at the concept from the metaphysical as well as linguistic angle. Despite such commonalities Bhartṛhari and Nyāya-Vaiśeṣika provide different grounds for their presuppositions about the reality of one and indivisible Time (*akhaṇḍakāla*). For the former *Kāla* is conceived as the power of *Brahman* that helps Bhartṛhari to make his non-dualistic stand tenable. He needed a concept that could explain the phenomena of multiplicity and change that is the benchmark of the empirical world.

Kāla serves more as a principle that projects the *Brahman* as the process of the world (*jagat prakriyā*). With the notion of *Kāla* as a power Bhartṛhari very cogently delineates how there is constant change and activity in the empirical level, as every object of the world goes through beginning, sustenance and destruction; hence change. But in consonance with his non-dualistic philosophy he finally discards the reality of *Kāla* as a separate principle. Here the power (*śakti*) and the wielder of power lose their separate identity. So the arguments of Bhartṛhari for the eternality, indivisibility and pervasiveness of *Kāla* are not based on inference or causality as it is the case with Nyāya-Vaiśeṣika. They on the other hand accept the empirical world as real and use the concept of *akhaṇḍakāla* to explain the relativity of the temporal concepts (*khaṇḍakāla*). But if we look little deeper it may be discovered that both the systems of ontology even though structured on opposite foundation have a common approach to their analysis. Both admit that it is the language and the way we use it in ordinary communication can lead us up to a metaphysical stand. Maybe, one may offer different interpretations of such linguistic usages but that does not eradicate the importance of "language" as a phenomenon that helps in determining the metaphysical geography.

5

Time as a Mental Construct
Buddhism and Yoga

So far we have discussed the Bhartṛhari and Nyāya-Vaiśeṣika position on time (*kāla*) as an all-pervading, eternal and indivisible reality. *Kāla* is One and continuous. Now let us scan the opposite viewpoint that denies the eternality and all-pervasiveness to time. Time is just another name for a conglomeration of discreet yet indivisible units of time. The way the common man describes time as duration is also dismissed just as a mental construct (*viklapa*) or intellectual construct (*buddhi-kalpita*). Such a view is advocated, interestingly, by two schools of thought -- one non-Brāhmanic and the other Brāhmanic, subscribing to two distinct world-views. Time (*kāla*) for both the schools, viz. Buddhism and Yoga is a series of indivisible moments (*aṇu*) or point-instants (*kṣaṇa*s). The idea of time as receptacle of the objects of the empirical world (*jagaddhara*) is inconceivable in the metaphysical programme of either Buddhism or Yoga. Before I undertake more detailed discussion on these two philosophical positions let me make it clear that the word Buddhism is too sweeping a term. Buddhism is rather a generic name for divergent views developed through different phases of history. It branched into different and sometimes conflicting metaphysical systems. There are multiple branches of Buddhism that sometimes holds unto radically diverse world-views. My aim in this work is not to cover the entire range of views available in different branches of Buddhism. Rather my objective is to contrast and compare Bhartṛhari's conception of time as power with the alternative models, offered by certain schools of philosophy. So I shall be mainly concentrating on Sautrāntrika-Yogācāra Buddhism advocated by Diṅnāga, Kamalaśīla, Śāntarakṣita and others. Besides, Bhartṛhari in his Kālasamuddeśa also refers to these alternative views, viz. time as substance and time as moment as expounded by Vaiśeṣika and the Sautrantrika school of Buddhism, respectively. We have seen in the previous chapter how divergent ontological viewpoints converge at certain points on certain issues, in this chapter too we would be looking into two opposing metaphysical systems, one nominalistic and the other realistic, coming together when it comes to the question of analysis of time as a concept. Sautrāntrika Buddhism is definitely not a realistic system in the usual sense of the term, but Yoga system is realistic as far as its metaphysical position is concerned; yet both delineate time and temporality as the handiwork of our intellect. It would be still more fascinating to note that when it comes to the question of time-divided (*khaṇḍakāla*), especially the ideas of past, present and future, how the boundaries between ontological systems almost fall apart. I intend to address this particular issue in the next chapter.

Time as Point-Instant: Buddhism

The problem of life, change and world gets a sort of revolutionary treatment in the works of the Buddhist scholars of various denominations. But a close look at the development of their philosophical ideas seems to be rooted in two basic ideas provided by the original Buddhism. They are *anitya* (impermanence) and *anātma* (no soul). In Buddhism the concept of time evolved from the emphasis on change. This finds reflection in the idea of *anitya*. The doctrine of universal momentariness (Kṣaṇabhaṅgavāda) can be said to be a corollary of the theory of *anitya*. Again, the theory of momentariness has received various interpretations from the Buddhist philosophers of different schools in its different periods of development. According to Buddhism impermanence is the fundamental principle. So the reality is seen as dynamic. Full manifestation of this idea is developed in the Sautrāntrika–Yogācāra school of Vasubandhu, Diṅnāga, Kamalaśīla and Śāntarakṣita. They resurrect the theory of Kṣaṇabhaṅgavāda and Anityavāda of the older Buddhism and provide it a new texture. For Yogācāra Buddhism the reality is a flux or flow. The static is only momentary, not in the continuing present, except in the sense that moments are surrounded by the continuum,

> as it might be a mountain torrent flowing swiftly from afar and carrying everything along with it, and there is no moment, pause or minute (*khano, layo, muhutto*) in which it comes to rest.[1]

Thus, the principles of change and impermanence lead to a revolutionary interpretation of the ontological world-view, making Buddhism stands apart from all other philosophical traditions, both Brāhmanical and non-Brāhmanical.

According to Sautrāntrika–Yogācāra Buddhism (hence forward would be referred by the generic name Buddhism) there can be no eternal and non-caused entity. The so-called static and eternal entities like God, time or space are ideal fictions (*samvṛttas*), pure and simple. As the world is characterized by change we have to first of all understand why there is change. Change is not modification but destruction of the one moment and substitution of one moment by another. An entity perishes and is replaced by another at every instant. This destruction is total and spontaneous. With this the Buddhists refute the Nyāya-Vaiśeṣika theory that the

1 Quoted from Coomaraswamy 1992: 159.

object continues to be the same but there is change only in the condition and quality. Buddhists argue: does the change represent something different from the thing changing or is it the thing itself? If change is nothing different, then the thing will continue in the same state, i.e. the thing will remain as it is. So there will be no change. If it is something different it will continue to remain different; and again, there will be no change. So we are bound to admit that there is another object at every consecutive moment. If the milk is changed to curd, the Nyāya-Vaiśeṣika would assume that the matter is same but the conditions change. But Buddhists argue that either a substance remains the same or it becomes something different. It cannot be both – changing and at the same time remaining the same. The idea of time as instant and its inseparability from being – as instantaneous – is the key to the Buddhist conceptual structure.

Diṅnāga in the introductory passage of his treatise *Pramāṇa-Samuccaya* states that the external world that we experience has a double dimension. One is dependent on our sense. This sensible world is momentary. The other is how it is grasped by our understanding. Through the reproductive power of understanding (imagination) we construct the idea of objects and events with duration. We as if freeze the momentary sense data into a durable piece and give it a name (*vikalpa*). All the things that we experience through senses are nothing but a string of moments. Kamalaśīla elaborating this idea states that momentariness is the fundamental character of the world of experience. The concept is applicable to both, matter and mind alike as both are taken to be momentary. According to the Buddhists the reality is a ceaseless flow of moments. There is neither being nor not-being but only becoming. "Everything is momentary – *sarvam kṣaṇikam*" is said to be the roaring of the *saugata* lion. Two classical examples are offered to explain the theory – the stream of a river and the flame of a lamp. This thesis repudiates the reality of anything conceived to be permanent – be it God or matter or the self. Along with this the ideas of duration, extension, permanence and continuity are rejected dialectically in consonance with their principal theses.

Despite the momentary nature of the world it is normal for human beings, engaged in the pursuit of his daily activity, to talk of existence and non-existence of things he encounters in the course of his daily experience. Thus he has a tendency to label anything as real that has some practical use for him.[2] But the Buddhists advocate that such real (so-called) objects that have some purposive action cannot be anything than instantaneous flashes. They are momentary. So such real things that are of some purposive use (*artha-kriyākārī-rūpa*) in empirical life, in reality, are instantaneous. Such realities do not exist as objective realities, as the connotation of reality is causal efficiency (*arthakriyākāritva*). Causal efficiency is the very basis of mapping of the reality as series of moments. Therefore, according to the Buddhists the connotation of reality is causal efficiency. But it is only the last moment of the series of moments that accounts for the efficiency. The seed is turned into sprout, due to the last moment of the seed, not those moments when it is in the granary. The seed is changing every moment otherwise it would be dormant and never change into the sprout. The former moments cannot overlap the moment of efficiency, still less can its future moments produce the preceding effect. To be efficient it has to depend on the last moment. But the moment of the causal efficiency is also the totality of causes and conditions owing to which it exists. The moment we consider to be real is the moment when action (i.e. the flow of moments) is finished.[3] Śāntarakṣita claims that

[2] *yad eva padārthajatām . . . tatraiva vastu vyavasthā*. Here *vastu* means that which are efficient. See Stcherbatsky 2008: 81.

[3] *kriyāparisamāpti lakṣaṇa eva eṣo naḥ kṣaṇaḥ*, quoted in ibid.: 82.

the essence of reality is motion, viz. the flow of moments. Causality, the interdependence of moments following one another, evokes the illusion of stability and duration. So the reality is dynamic without any real enduring substance in them. But the opponents may raise two vital criticisms. It may be argued that (a) the thing may exercise its power, i.e. produce its effect gradually and not all at once, so that it may last for several moments or a period of time; or (b) it may be that it possesses the power but it does not exercise it. Its power remains latent, owing to some factors which hinder it from being exercised. The Buddhists successfully refute both these criticisms by countering that in either case one has to assume that the cause waits for some other factors in order to produce its own effect. But if it waits for some other factor, then by itself it has no causal power. For instance, if the cause is *C* and it has the power to produce the effect *E*, *A* will produce *E* in the very first moment of its existence. If, however, *C* waits for *D* in order to produce *E*, we should say that *C* does not have the power to produce *E* by itself, which contradicts the original hypothesis. On the other hand, if it is presumed that *C* cannot produce *E*, because *D* obstructs this causal efficiency, then, the Buddhists argue, it would be better in that case to say that the causal power does not belong to *C* by itself, but belongs to *C* together with the absence of *D*. To sum up the argument, the cause cannot be conceived as merely latent power or a power which is yet to be exercised. If something has power, that power must be at once exercised, and if it is at once exercised, the thing would cease to exist in the next moment. So it would be absurd to say that anything may last forever. Thus the permanent coincides with the non-efficient, i.e. the unreal.

So far we have seen how the Buddhists successfully argue that there cannot be an enduring entity that changes. On the similar ground the Buddhists argue that it would be untenable to say that there is a substance called Time. With this they discard the Nyāya-Vaiśeṣika thesis that time is a substance. The criterion that distinguishes the real from the fictitious is causal efficiency. In other words that which is real is essentially of the nature of a cause, i.e. it gives rise to effects. This happens as if in the womb of the moments. So there is constant change which alone is the basic feature of our experienceable world. Momentariness means change; and existence signifies efficiency. Therefore causal efficiency is restricted only to the momentary; the permanent cannot be causally efficient. The Buddhist points out that causal efficiency can be exercised in either of the two conceivable ways, viz. in succession or simultaneity, and that the idea of the permanent is incompatible with it. If it exercises causal efficiency in the very first moment, can the permanent be said to exist after that? If so, it would give rise to the same effects in the second and in all succeeding moments, ad infinitum. This would lead to an absurdity. If it does not produce effects and yet is imagined to be existent, it would then have two contradictory qualities, being efficient in the first moment and non-efficient in other moments. This manifest difference in the nature of the reality (moments) points to the fact that the entity in question cannot be the same as that of the previous moment. The Buddhist dictum is: that cannot be one, about which one could predicate contradictory characteristics. In other words, to say that the real or the efficient exercises its causal power in the very first moment of its existence is as good as saying that in the succeeding moment it would cease to exist. Efficiency cannot be attributed to a durable or permanent entity. With this argument the Buddhist proceeds to show that the permanent can never be said to exercise efficiency successively. If the permanent has the power to give rise to effects in succession, it may be asked whether during its execution of present efficiency it also has the past and future efficiencies as well. If it has, the Buddhist argues, the inevitable result is that it would exercise them at the same moment – thus resulting in simultaneous production. If it does not have the past and the future efficiencies, it can never produce the effects. Thus the present only has causal efficiency and not the future and the past. To say that the entity continues to be the same through past, present and future moments is to commit the fallacy – as pointed out before – of investing it with contradictory qualities, which dismisses its identity. Therefore at no two moments can the entity remain the same.

Explicating their position further Dharmakīrti clarifies that we must not confuse causality with real production. It is only a functional interdependence. The cause being momentary does not produce the effect. The cause merely precedes the effect and the effect merely follows the cause. Existence is efficiency and efficiency is the cause. Things arise neither out of self nor out of not-self; nor out of both, nor out of neither. Everything produced is destroyed. That which comes into existence and then ceases to exist is called momentary. But *kṣaṇa* is not a time-moment. Things only appear to exist for a moment. That is why it is called *kṣaṇika*. So the distinction we ordinarily entertain between persons and objects is entirely the product of intellect. It is the creation of language. Though ultimately unreal, this distinction is needed in the empirical world because that is how language is used in case of human communication. Thus in this scheme of metaphysics duration and continuity are nothing but conceptual constructions. The notion of duration formed of a chain of successive moments is merely metaphorical, devoid of any reality.

Not only the Buddhists refute the possibility of the real "duration", they also discard the view that "Time" is the receptacle of the events and objects. Time cannot be separated from the objects that exist in them. As the receptacle (*ādhāra*) of objects it has no separate causal efficiency (*arthakriyākāritva*). In our day-to-day life we come to believe that things happen *in* time. But this is not the true representation of the reality.

In this case our faculty of productive imagination (*kalpanā*) is at work. So we distinguish between an object and its receptacle. Again, we use such durational concepts as "day", "hour", "month", etc. This is due to our mental attitude which uses the faculty of constructive imagination. Even the moment as such is not graspable by our immediate sense-perception. Such notions of duration are untenable.

> If a thing exists at a moment *A*, it cannot also exist at the same moment *B*, for to exist really at the moment *A* means not to have existence at the moment *B* or at any other moment. If we thus admit that the same thing continues to exist at the moment *B*, this could only mean that it at once really exists and does not really exist at the moment *A*. If a thing could have real duration through several moments, it would represent real unity existing at once at different times. Either is the enduring entity a fiction and real is only the moments, or the moments are fictions and real is only duration. For the Buddhists, the moments alone are real, duration is fiction, for if it were a reality, it would be really existing at different times at once, i.e. existing and at the same time not existing at a given moment.[4]

Thus the ultimate reality is timeless, not in the sense of an eternal being, but in the sense of having no real duration. It is a mathematical point-instant that itself is immeasurable.

Our direct perception also proves that there is nothing called "time" as such. Our experience of the direct perception proves the Buddhist point. All our sense experiences are nothing more than sensory moments. The duration of objects beyond that moment of sensation cannot be guaranteed by the sensation itself. For example, we experience a blue patch but never the blue object. To say something is perceived as blue object we have to imagine a continued existence of quality

---

4 Stcherbatsky 2008: 86-87.

of blueness in a substance. But our direct experience of the sensations reveals that we can at best seize the present moment. This makes it clear that all objects that have causal efficiency are momentary experiences. It is our imagination that constructs the concept of object, when stimulated by sensation.

We have gathered from the above arguments that for the Buddhists the notion of time is a fiction constructed by our understanding out of flashes of moments. As time is neither perceivable nor inferable, temporality cannot be expressed in words or language. The so-called temporal experience can at best be described by such words as "this", "now", etc. Diṅnāga while analysing the nature of reality argues that the reality is nothing more than point-instants or *svalakṣaṇa*s. Such point-instants are thing-in-itself that can neither be defined nor measured. So there is no real continuity and duration. The homogeneous succession, where the posterior moment resembles the antecedent, gives rise to the notion of so-called duration. In reality, this similarity is no continuity of an identical entity, but is due to a lack of perception of the subtle distinction of similar moments. But in a heterogeneous succession the difference is greater, and therefore the discontinuity is noticed, which is technically called the production of a dissimilar moment (*vijātīya kṣaṇa utpāda*). This is how the ideas of duration and substance are accounted for from the empirical standpoint. *Svalakṣaṇa*s are "the only thing in the universe which is a non-construction, a non-fiction". At this point one may argue that how can we account for the notion of time in terms *svalakṣaṇa* which are immeasurable and ineffable? Diṅnāga argues back that *svalakṣaṇa* is the *shortest possible* time. This is at best understandable in terms of mathematical point instants. There is nothing unusual about such an idea of time as "point-instant", since such a notion of time has been used in astronomical science.[5] In fact, in our ancient

[5] *jyotirvidyāsiddha* – quoted in Stcherbatsky 2008: 106.

scientific tradition a distinction is made between the gross time (*sthūlakāla*) and subtle time (*sūkṣmakāla*). The astronomers make subtle time the basis of all calculations about the planetary movements. The subtle time is an indivisible "time particular" that does not contain any parts that can be understood in terms of sequence.[6] According to the Indian astronomers the motion of a thing during a single moment is the "motion of just that time",[7] i.e. not of another moment, not of another time. This time is nothing but differential of a planet's longitude. So there is nothing wrong, Buddhists argue, in admitting that time is nothing but such mathematical point-instants. This reality can be neither described nor named. It can at best be uttered as "this" or "now". Such point-instants, in fact, are ineffable and unnameable. Whatever is nameable is a thought construction.[8]

This specific formulation of the idea of time as instant is intimately related to the Buddhist conception of cause. But in this case causation implies functional dependence. A non-cause is equivalent to the non-existent. That which is real/existent must be causally efficient, and it is only the instantaneous which can be so. Time as instant, again, indicates this ever-fluctuating, evanescent character of being with which it is fused ontologically. Being, time and causality form a conceptual whole in Buddhist thinking. The protest against the substance-view is there at the very root of Buddhist thinking.

Time as Atom: Yoga

Yoga conception of time is quite atypical. As a system of philosophy it claims to share the ontological scheme of its ally, viz. the Sāṁkhya. Surprisingly, when it comes to the conception of time the Yoga system seems to part company with the

---

6 *pūrva apara-bhāga-vikala* – Stcherbatsky 2008: 106.

7 *tatkāliki gatiḥ* – ibid.

8 *sabda vikalpa yonaḥ, vikalpaḥ śabda-yonaḥ* – ibid.

Sāṁkhya. In the Sāṁkhya format of metaphysics time is not real since it is no distinct entity in addition to the twenty-five fundamental principles enlisted by it. In fact, the older Sāṁkhya straightforward dismisses the reality of time. But some later versions of Sāṁkhya offer some status to time by admitting it as *ākāśā*, itself. As opposed to this stand we come across a detailed discussion about time in Yoga. This system of thought conceives time as a series of continuous moments. The exact position may be deciphered from the following commentary of Patañjali's *Yoga-Sūtra* III.52:

kṣaṇa tat kramayoḥ saṁyamat vivejam jñānam

> By *saṁyama* (concentration) over Moment and its Succession, [one] comes the discriminative knowledge.
>
> As an atom is the minutest particle of the matter, so also a Moment (*kṣaṇa*) is minutest time. Or a Moment is that much of time which a moving atom takes to reach a position different from its previous one. The uninterrupted flow is thereof is a succession (*karma*). There is no real togetherness of a moment and its succession. *Muhūrtta* (48 minutes), day, night, etc. are conceptual (imaginary) aggregates. Such time is unsubstantial, a mental construct and a mere verbal idea. To ordinary persons it seems to be an objective reality. The moment, however pertains to whatever is real (*vastupatita*) and is determined by succession, and succession consists in sequence of moments. The *yogīs* who know time call it by the name Time. Further, two moments do not co-exist. Nor can there be any succession of two co-existing moments, for that is impossible. The sequence of posterior moment from the one that precedes is Succession. Therefore, only one moment is present. The antecedent and the later moments do not exist, and hence, there is no combination of them. The so-called past and future moments should be explained as connected with change. For this reason, the whole universe

> undergoes change in that one moment; all the characteristics (*dharma*) are installed on that single moment. . . .[9]

From the above commentary it is clear Yoga ontology does not dismiss time as unreal unlike its metaphysical ally. The time is real not as an infinite dimension but as a "moment". Time is real not in the sense that it is infinite but infinitesimal. It is atomic and dynamic. It is not to be conceived as an incalculably small quantum of time taken out of infinite duration. Nor is it to be understood as a mere determination of time dependent upon relation to an external limiting condition (*upādhi*), as is held by the Vaiśeṣika. Time is neither infinite nor a chunk of determinate time like hour or a day. Both the views refer to time as static. Both the ideas refer to magnitude. But anything that has magnitude is bound to be static. But what is called time is never static. It flows or passes. Therefore, time should be conceived as infinitesimal. We must keep in mind that Yoga does not hold time to be series of moments. Moments do not exist together but one after another. Moment can exist only by superseding the one preceding it. This order of their being is called succession. Two moments cannot coexist. It is not possible for moments to be actually strung together in a linear arrangement, for when one of them is, others are not. The continuity of time should therefore be explained in terms of an ideal series of moments. It is the intellect which pieces together the moments – the existent present, and the non-existent past and future. Every moment, being immediately subsequent to that has just passed off and being also the only moment of the time of its existence, is necessarily the present moment.

Again, there can be no combination or aggregation of moments as they never coexist. Moments exist one after another. This ordering of moments is called succession. But

[9] *kṣaṇabhedastu yogibuddhigamya eva. . . .* – *Yoga-Sūtra* III.53, trans. quoted from Sen 1968: 516.

the moment and its succession also cannot coexist. Nor also moments contain succession as its characteristic. For, succession implies a relation (of the prior with the posterior). But the relation in this case is no part of the relata. So succession itself is rather a conceptual rather than real. Vijñānabhikṣu argues that there is no proof for the existence of an eternal and infinite time (*mahākāla*). A moment is described to be *vastupatita*. Vācaspati Miśra interprets the word as signifying *vāstava* (real), whereas Vijñānabhikṣu means by the term that "which is included in the category of reality" *vastukotau praviṣṭhaḥ* or as objective (*vastubhūta*).[10] So we can gather that for followers of the Yoga system of philosophy the moment or the time-atom is not a mere abstraction or logical figment, it has a reality of its own.

Further, according to Yoga, though time is infinitesimal and there is no observable succession, the moment is not static. It represents a single unit of actual change which the whole material order undergoes. So it follows that as each moment is an independent entity, the absolute and irreducible unit of time, it is the measure of the minimal positional change in nature, i.e. of the movement of an atom from its own position to the next. So it is dynamic. At the same time it is essential to the nature of moments that they should arise, one after another in uninterrupted succession. Vyāsa in his *Bhāṣya* on *Yoga-Sūtra*, therefore, defines a moment (*kṣaṇa*) as the

> ultimate minimum of time, and cannot further be divided up . . . and continuous flow of moments is their course (*karma*). . . . Their uninterrupted course is what is called "time". The whole world passes through a mutation in any one moment; so all the external qualities of the world are related to this present moment.[11]

---

[10] Sen 1968: 519.

[11] Coomaraswamy 1990: 9.

The present time is real though imperceptible; and time has no reality apart from the imperceptible atomic present. Vyāsa further says:

> Moments and the sequence of this cannot be combined into real (*vastu*). Thus, time being of this nature, does not correspond to anything real, but is a product of mind, and flows as a result of perception or of words.[12]

But the moment is objective and rests on sequence.[13]

Time, as we have seen, can be connected with change. But time is not at all explicitly identified with change in the Yoga system of thought. It is succession that is held to be determined by change or activity.[14] The whole universe undergoes change but such a change can be assigned to each moment that is the present moment.[15] The past and the future moments are non-existent as independent entities, though they form part of change that the world undergoes. At the same time we come across very interesting account of the nature of such divisions of time as past, present and future which would be dealt little later.

Patañjali in his *Bhāṣya* has already talked about the omniscience that results from concentration (*saṁyama*) on moments and their succession. This yogic concentration means knowing the three forms of time, viz. past, present and future at one moment non-successively. So what is negated in such experience is not the negation of the moment but succession of moments. In reality, time just consists of one moment. It is

---

12 *sa khalvayam kālo vastuśūnyo 'pi buddhinirmāṇaḥ śabdajñānānupāti* (*Yoga Bhāṣya*), quoted in Sharma 1972: 22.

13 *kṣaṇastu vastupatita kramābalambi* – ibid.

14 *Yogasūtra*, IV.33: . . . *pariṇāma-aparānta nigrahayaḥ kraman* (succession is ascertained by the cessation of change).

15 *ekena kṣaṇena kr̥tsno lokaḥ pariṇāmam anubhabati* – Commentary on *Yogasūtra* III.52, Prasad 1992: 518.

due to the lack of real knowledge that ordinary persons perceive time as infinite series of present moments emerging out of future moments and vanishing into the past moments. According to *Yoga-Bhāṣya*, the continuity of time, whether finite or infinite, is only a convenient fiction derived from a conceptual fusion of "real" moments. Nothing can be less like our consciousness of time than a fictitious series of moments; nor does our perceptual experience know anything of moments of a mathematical sort.

As Yoga system shares Sāṁkhya metaphysics, naturally the question arises about the status of the two metaphysical principles concerned, viz. *puruṣa* and *prakṛti* vis-à-vis the notion of time as a moment. The adherents of this system of thought would say that the concept of time is inapplicable to both the metaphysical principles. They are timeless. Time stands for modification. *Puruṣa*, the principle of pure intelligence being immutatable can only be conceived as beyond time. So also is *prakṛti*. Being the ultimate material cause of the evolutes that constitute the objective world it cannot be subsumed under any of its evolutes. If we admit that time is real and objective following Vācaspati Miśra and Vijñānabhikṣu, then also time is nothing but a part of *prakṛti* in its manifested form. But as the un-manifested principle, *prakṛti* lies outside the pale of time. Hence it is also timeless and eternal.

The Atomic View of Time: Two Dimensions

So far we have examined two philosophical systems that view time as an atomic reality. At certain points both the theories seem almost moving in a parallel course. For example, both the systems of thought dismiss the eternality and unity (oneness) of time; and instead they grant reality only to the moment; both take for granted that sequence (*krama*) of moments is nothing more than a mental construct; again, both depict the moment as dynamic; and finally both the doctrines negate reality of past and future elements, thus reposing the power to the present alone. Here we notice two distinct metaphysical schemes converge in their depiction of time as atomic in nature. Yet a look at their metaphysical structure reveals how distanced are they in their approach to their world-view. Sautrāntrika–Yogācāra Buddhism is based on two basic pillars of Buddhism in general, viz. *anitya* and *anātma*. Yoga, on the other hand, true to its Brāhmanical allegiance, would neither admit the flux nor the impermanence as ultimate truth. *Puruṣa* and *prakṛti* along with *Īśvara* (God) are fundamental to its explication of the empirical world. These three principles are eternal and timeless. Therefore, the atomic time, though real is not the reality. Time as an instant in the Yoga philosophy is based on a different ontological scheme. The graded evolutes of *prakṛti*, including individual soul, mind and material objects are in no way mental constructs or *buddhi-nirmāṇa*.

As Pariṇāmavādins they subscribe to the theory that *prakṛti* as the material cause evolves into a real world. The momentary character of time does not hold true of the Reality. Their analysis of the creation as *pariṇāma* reveals that the principle *prakṛti* that manifests itself as the empirical world is existent so that it could support the process of evolution and involution. So the empirical world is not finally analysed in terms of the series of moments. But the Sautrāntrika Yogācāra is based on the opposite metaphysical presupposition. They defy eternalism and naïve realism of Sāṁkhya-Yoga in every respect. The empirical world is a flux; and the so-called self, mind and material object are nothing but *kalpanā*. So time seen as a *kṣaṇa* is of the nature of mathematical point-instant (*svalakṣaṇa*) that plays a fundamental role in their metaphysics. In the Buddhist scheme of thought time as an instant *svalakṣaṇa*, implies the notion of time as instantaneous being. This understanding of time and being is a radical departure from the Sāṁkhya-Yoga way of conceiving the reality. If Yoga emphasizes on *nityatā* of the realities, the Buddhists work out a philosophy of *anitya*. In the Yoga system time as an instant does not imply the instantaneousness of the Being. Time as an instant and the instantaneity of the Being are two distinct concepts. Yoga rather brings out a distinction between *dharma* (the qualities that is constantly changing into another) and *dharmin* (the substance that implies permanence). The Being or substance is conceived to be enduring and persisting through change. No doubt, Yoga talks of the atomicity of moments, but they are not the series of moments but discreet moments. Obviously such a notion of time is introduced to explain the change in the empirical level, for each moment is the present moment which accounts for the change. The Buddhism, on the other hand, denies existence to anything else than the point-instants. So it leaves no room for the category of existence. We have already noted that for Buddhism what is existent is causally efficient; and what is causally efficient is instantaneous in character.

In this context it would be interesting to bring in for discussion another philosophical position that too holds time as atomic in nature. In the Jaina metaphysical scheme, time is regarded as an instant. This instant is objective as well as real. Time is a mono-dimensional and asymmetrical series constituted of time atoms (*kālāṇu*). The conventional time periods that we talk of in our usages are dependent on external factors such as any standard motion. It is thus relative and conditional aspect dependent on extraneous factors whereas the real objective atoms are discrete and in reality can never be combined. Again, the Jaina conception of time should not be confused with the Yoga or the Buddhist conception of time. For the Jainas the time is not only atomic and objective but also eternal. Neither beginning nor end could be ascribed to it. The *aṇus* of the *kāla* are many, conceived in a linear order.

6

The Concept of Khaṇḍakāla
The Divisible Time

BHARTṚHARI as well as the Vaiśeṣika system of thought have admitted eternality and conceptual independence to time as a reality. On the other hand, Buddhism as well as Yoga view time as unique atomic moments and duration as unreal mental construct (*buddhi-kalpita*). The difference in their conception of time as a principle is ultimately determined by the ontological structure each of these systems adopts. But whatever be the nature of the objective world as such, be it real or be it ideal or else a flux, it cannot be denied that we as human beings encounter the events and actions in the world, and also think and speak about them. Such acts are crucial to our life as without such acts we would be no better than a log of wood or piece of stone. But to think and speak about the world we need to place them in time order, viz. past, present and future. So, most of the systems of thought admits that we cannot avoid talking about time as far as our thought and speech are concerned. Our thought is ordered in sequence of the past, present and future. Similarly, our speech is characterized by the use of the tense – past, present and future. Without such an order our speech would be a jumbled mass. So whether *Kāla* is accepted as real or imaginary, we have to admit division of time (*khaṇḍakāla*) at least in terms of past, present and future. The conceptual compulsion on the part of the philosophers is very fittingly pointed out by P.K. Mukhopadhyaya:

> In India there are many systems of thought, such as Buddhism, that do not admit the reality of time. But it is admitted on all hands that our everyday as well as theoretical language is replete with words that somehow involve reference to time or use of temporal words. The systems that do not admit the reality of time also feel obliged to provide a good explanation – though not justification since it is not possible on the view that time is not real – of these usages. Those, who, on the other hand admit time to be an item of reality, justify the usages in question by pointing at the fact that the experience that the usages is incontrovertible. However, as could be naturally expected, those who do not admit the reality of time have disputed this claim. But there is no dispute about the fact that the usages in question are there and every theory is under obligation to offer or cite, if and when challenged, some good explanation (self-developed or borrowed) of this fact that would be also consistent with their theory. But to provide certain good explanation of certain group of usages seems to be the primary task of the disciplines of language study such as linguistics, semantics, etc.[1]

Interestingly, though most of the philosophical schools admit that it is almost impossible to repudiate the significance of such divisions as far as our description of the experience of the empirical world is concerned, there is no unanimity of opinion among the philosophers regarding the status of the past, present and future; some only admitting the priority to the present and some others only to past and future. In this chapter, I would like to focus on this interesting issue with special reference to the three models of thought I have discussed earlier – Nyāya-Vaiśeṣika, Buddhism/Yoga and Bhartṛhari.

It must be stated at the outset that though we come across three conceptual models as far as Time as a principle is

---

[1] Mukhopadhyaya 2009: 60-61.

concerned (apart from the fourth that totally denies the reality of time, viz. Advaita, Mādhyamika), none of the systems of thought is ready to admit the reality (in the philosophical sense) of the measurable time. Such division of time, in most cases is taken to be conventional or artificial. This is so because though we talk of the past, present and future, or for that matter quick or slow such divisions of time are not measurable in terms of Time. Time itself cannot be used to measure relative temporal duration. In other words Time cannot be used to measure "time-word", like slow, fast, past, present and future, whereas such words are expressive of measurable magnitude. The reason why Time (*akhaṇḍakāla*) as a principle cannot be used for measuring duration is that it is unlimited. Only those things that have limits are measurable. As unlimited space is not measurable, we have to use a metre scale that is limited in dimension, to measure the relative distance of things in space. Similarly, we use such units of measure as "day" or "year" to measure the relative events in time. So our usage of different times or periods of time forces us to realize that *one* time is used as different times, artificially created by convention. Therefore Bhartṛhari as well as Nyāya-Vaiśeṣika talk of two types of time – one, the real, eternal and uncreated time (*mahākāla*) and the other, an imaginary time (*kalpita kāla/ khaṇḍakāla*). Despite such unanimity one comes across very interesting debate about the concept of *khaṇḍakāla* or *kalpita kāla*.

Bhartṛhari on Division of Time

We have already discussed about Bhartṛhari's views about such division of time like – prior–posterior, day and month, moments and Manu's age (the longest duration of time) while elaborating his notion of Time as a power. So here I shall concentrate on his conception of the past, present and future. The reason for highlighting on this dimension of time may be assigned to the fascination of different philosophical schools about the relative priority of the one over the other.

Bhartṛhari introduces the notion of the division of time into past, present and future in the 37th *kārikā* of Kālasamuddeśa in the following way:

> *kriyopādhiśca san bhūtobhabiṣyadvartamānatāḥ* ।
> *ekadaśābhirakarai vibhaktāḥ pratipadyate* ॥

> Time having activity as its superimposition, becomes past, future and present, that are divided into eleven forms.

Helārāja elucidating the *kārikā* says:

> When the activities are created and later on destroyed, then (time) having these activities as superimposition, is designated as past time. But, when activities have their means nearby and when their emergence is expected, then time having these (activities) as superimposition, becomes future. But (time) having begun and not completed activity as its superimposition (is) called present.

In the above *kārikā* the word *kriyopādhi* is of eminent importance. The division of time – be it between the "prior" and "posterior", be it between the difference of "hours" and "seasons" or be it between the "past", "present" and "future" – is not a constituent of the eternal Time that he calls as *Kālaśakti*. It is due to the actions (*kriyā*) of the empirical world, that we experience time as limited (*upādhi*) and hence divided.

Clarifying his position as a non-dualist who has so far projected *Kālaśakti* as One and indivisible Bhartṛhari in the 49th *kārikā* declares:

> *ekasya śaktayastisraḥ kālasya samavasthitāḥ* ।
> *yat sambandhena bhāvanāṁ darśanādarśane śatam* ॥

> Time which is One has three powers on account of which appearance and disappearance of objects take place.

The above *kārikā* presents the past, present and future not as the division of Time but the power (*śakti*) or (we may say the function) of the Time. Time hides (in fact, he uses the word *adr̥śyate*) the objects with the help of the two of these powers (past and future) and projects one (*dr̥śyate*), i.e. the power called present. We notice here that Bhartr̥hari marks out the "present" as something directly experienceable or visible (*dr̥śyate*). On the other hand, the past and future are put in a separate category "something that is hidden" (*adr̥śyate*). So ultimately we find that the past, present and future can be connected with the two primary functions of Time as a *śakti* – *abhyanujñā* and *pratibandha*. We also must note the use of another unusual word in the above-mentioned *kārikā*, viz. *śakti*, with reference to the past, present and future. It seems that he uses the word *śakti* rather generously. In Kālasamuddeśa even the old age (*jarā*) is called a power of Time apart from the three. We may guess that perhaps he sees no contradiction in postulating "power" in the case of past, present and future, because earlier he has stated that Time (*Kālaśakti*), though conceived as a power, is identical with the wielder of the power, viz. *śabdatattva*. I have stated earlier that *śakti* also connotes potentiality. So we are not sure in what sense exactly he uses the time *śakti* with reference to the past, present and future. Whatever might be his reason for the use of the word *śakti* we find that all powers, including the powers of threefold time, can be said to be finally identical with the ultimate Reality. They are perceived as empirically real though their effects are mutually exclusive. Bhartr̥hari justifies his position regarding the division of time in the 48th *kārikā* of Kālasamuddeśa in the following way:

tasyabhinnasya kālasya vyavahāre kriyākr̥tāḥ ।
bheda iva taryaḥ siddha yaṁlloko nātivartate ॥

Of this Time which is One, three divisions, as it were, are brought about in actual practice by actions, the three divisions the world cannot ignore.

This is evident from the above line that we cannot do without the division of time when it comes to the level of our practical life (*vyavahāra*) which is based on our experience as well as the expressions of our thought about the world, in which we live in. Here the word *vyavahāra* implies the way we experience the events of the world and speak about them. In fact, the necessity for bringing in the notion of time lies with our speech pattern. Our experiences are arranged in the sequence of time and finally expressed in the form of their placement in the divided time; otherwise our communication about the phenomenal world would be impossible. Another important term used in the above-mentioned *kārikā* is *kriyākṛtaḥ*. Thus the notion of *kriyā* in the level of the experienceable world, and verbs implying *kriyā* in the level of utterance, are the most important concepts that reveal the significance of the division of time. According to Bhartṛhari the most important components of our utterances are the verbs implying action. Similarly, the most important way of looking at the phenomenal world is through actions. It is the actions that make the world change. No object is permanent or eternal. Here Bhartṛhari is approaching the riddle of the division of Time that is claimed to be indivisible, both as a metaphysician and also as a philosopher of language. The compulsions of our linguistic usage and *vyavahāra* of the empirical world conditioned by action that Time is stated to attain the division in the form of past, present and future. When the activities are created and later on destroyed, it is called the past. But when the activities are yet to occur, it is called the future. When the activity has begun and not yet completed is called the present.[2] Therefore even those schools of thought as Yoga and Sautrāntrika that conceive time as a mental construct cannot deny that we have to use our speech in terms of time divisions. Bhartṛhari pointing out the nature of such compulsion claims:

---

[2] III.9.37-38.

> Whether it is a construction of mind or it has an existence outside the mind, the expression in word is not possible without recourse to the notion of time.[3]

In this aspect one notices a strong influence of Patañjali, the grammarian. He explicitly mentions that the division of time into day and night, months and year is only an artificial way of calculation. Such calculations may be due to its conjunction with the movement of the sun (*kāyā kriyāḥ ādityagatya*).[4] He is also of the opinion that the threefold division of time is only empirical in nature. Bhartṛhari explains this idea further in *kārikā*s 6-8 of his Kālasamuddeśa.

Though in our philosophical discussion "present" is a problematic issue, but from the commonsensical point of view one may ask – how do we know about something which is no longer there and call it a past? To such a query, Bhartṛhari answers as follows:

> The objects produced by the action that we call past are preserved in our memory. They are remembered and expressed in words as the past. Similarly, we can conceive of objects yet to come, viz. future, in the mind as clearly as a well-polished mirror.[5]

Thus Time is the background or the cause of everything in the universe. Bhartṛhari emphasizes on the notion of change to explicate his notion of the threefold division of time in the following manner:

> Just as the current of a river tosses about grass, leaves and creepers, in the same way, Time brings about changes in objects.[6]

---

3 *jñānānugatamsaktiṁ vā bāhyam vā satyataḥ sthitam* ।
kālātmānamanāśritya vyavahārtuṁ na śakyate ॥ – III.9.58

4 *Mahābhāṣya* on Pāṇini II.2.5.

5 III.9.40.

6 Ibid.

The current of river displaces certain objects and puts back others in their place. This is the result of the flow. Similarly, the flow of Time creates objects and brings about changes in other objects. Here we note that Bhartṛhari introduces the idea of the inevitability of the factor called "change" in the phenomenal world. The change is conditioned by sequence; and sequence means appearing and disappearing of the states of the objects. Such change in states can only be described in terms of past, present and future. The appearance and disappearance of the states of the objects are possible through two functions of Time, viz. permission and suspension. So Bhartṛhari says:

> Time hides objects with the help of the two of its powers; it is the power called present which manifests the object.[7]

The power called future does not stand in the way of the present which is associated with the beginning of the object. What is called future would in due course of change become present. So past does not stand in the way of the present. What is past is past. It dies and so cannot not become the present, whereas it is the future which in due course of time would become the present. So the past and future are like the darkness which cannot be perceived nor can directly be known. It is the present which is like light; for, it allows us to perceive the state of the object directly. In this context we come across a fine metaphor provided in the Vaibhāsika texts. Particles of dust are to be found on both the sides of the beam of light entering through the window. But whereas the dust in the beam is visible; the dust on the both sides of the beam is not visible. It is only inferred. This explains why the past and future, though not perceptible like the present, are existent; and their existence could be inferred from the present.

Sometimes, Bhartṛhari compares past, present and future to three paths on which the objects move without any

---

7 *Mahābhāṣya* on Pāṇini III.9.50.

confusion. What was first in the path called future enters the path called present and disappears in the path called past. Here he follows the Yoga school of thought in describing the objects having three states and three transformations (*avasthāpariṇāma*). But such division of time in no way makes any difference to Time as the eternal principle.

> The passing away of objects does not bring about passing away of Time. The road is not affected by any difference in the movement of the people who walk on it.[8]

These three powers, though always present, are co-ordinated and between them, they perform the function of revelation and obstruction; and thus bring about the sequence of the phenomena. With the help of these threefold division, the power called Time urges the phenomenal world to move ahead in sequence.

At this point Bhartṛhari anticipates the objection that both the past and future being of the opposite nature could not possibly be applied to the same object or fact. He clarifies that when the causes and conditions are ready and produce their effect, then the object becomes manifest, fulfils its purpose, it is called the present. When the causes cease to function and the object has fulfilled its work, it is no longer perceptible, this is said to be the past. When the causes of an object are not yet in a condition to produce it, this is called the future. Thus one and the same thing acquires different names on the basis of the external circumstances according to the presence and the absence of purposeful activity. It is that which fulfils the purposeful activity. Now the question may be raised – if the performance of the purposeful activity is the only criterion of the existence of objects, then how can we say that the past also exists, for, it does not do any purposeful activity? Bhartṛhari would say that the performance of the purposeful

---

8 *Mahābhāṣya* on Pāṇini III.9.74.

activity is not the only test of existence. We must keep in mind that all divisions of Time are unreal and based on actions which are brought about by it. Time itself is dynamic that constantly creates and destroys the course events at proper time. Through this process the world order is preserved. Even the movement of the stars and planets that is often taken as the means of measuring the time is itself the creation of Time.

From our discussion so far, it becomes obvious that Bhartṛhari handles the issue of *khaṇḍakāla* from the angle of both metaphysics and speech. Therefore, I would not like to subscribe to Helārāja's view on his commentary on III.9.48. Helārāja is of the opinion that the whole purpose of Bhartṛhari in analysing the concept of division of time is more grammatical than philosophical. No doubt, while explaining the nature of language a grammarian and a linguist have to handle the issue of the use of verb in different tenses, but philosophers too use linguistic concepts as a tool for explicating their philosophical position. In the first part of this chapter I have highlighted how linguistic usage plays an important role in philosophical explanation. Besides, from our discussion about the three models that deal with the notion of time this is evident that philosophers cannot ignore the fundamentality of linguistic usage in their analysis of time as a concept. Any philosophical system that includes the concept of Time within their ontological scheme shares Bhartṛhari's concern. The anxiety about explaining the "time-words" including the use of the past, present and future tenses in speech can also be noted in such philosophical systems as Nyāya-Vaiśeṣika, Yoga and Buddhism. It seems Helārāja, true to his grammatical tradition perhaps feels that a grammarian need not get too much involved in philosophical explorations. From our exposition of some of the classical systems of philosophy this is now evident that explication of Time has something to do with an understanding of how our language functions. In fact, the problem of Time as such is inextricably related to our use of language.

The Nyāya-Vaiśeṣika on Division of Time

Nyāya-Vaiśeṣika admits the empirical validity of threefold division of time – past, present and future. But the infinite and indivisible substance called *Kāla* is not subdivided to make our conception of the past, present and future possible. Such divisions are not therefore integral to it. It is conventional, and hence, artificial. Nyāya-Vaiśeṣikas provides, enough justifications for their claim. First, if the divisions of time were real then past, present and future would be numerically and essentially different from one another. As a result, certain duration of time which is now cognized as present would always continue to be so. It cannot be cognized as future before or as past afterwards. This type of perception of the duration of time would go against the empirical way of looking at the events of the world. Again, if it is claimed that the one and unitary Time possesses the three determinations – pastness, presentness and futurity, then it would contradict the original thesis that Time is unitary in nature. Time is conceived not only as unitary but indivisible too. We have already discussed their arguments in support of their view. If Time is indivisible then it cannot be characterized by determinations. Besides, their (pastness, presentness and futurity) coincidence would make all temporal distinctions impossible. An event could never be cognized as future and then past. But how do we describe Time as divided into different periods?

Nyāya-Vaiśeṣikas solve this riddle by arguing that the distinctions of time as past, present and future are derived from its association with the limiting adjuncts (*upādhi*) in the form of generated events (actions or objects), which could be posited as having finite duration. *Akhaṇḍakāla*, although functioning as the universal substratum of all that exists in the empirical level, by itself, is independent of all events happening in it. So *kriyā* consists of the series of movements (*kṣaṇa*s) of which, some are past, some are present and some are yet to come. The event that is stated to be "present" is dependent upon its relation to an action/event which has begun but not yet ended. Similarly, the "past" is the time associated with an event that has passed off, and the "future" is the time associated with an event that is yet to come. But Time as substance, according to Nyāya-Vaiśeṣika, cannot be limited by any external determination. So the distinctions of past, present and future cannot be a part of Time. So this threefold division is necessitated because in the empirical life we place our experiences about objects and events in certain order. This order is not provided by our sense-experience, for we can only experience the present, neither the past, nor the future. So such divisions are mental/conceptual constructs. They are called *kriyākalpitakāla*. Besides, we as human beings communicate about the objects and events of the world. Our speech would be impossible if we do not place the events in terms of past, present and future. So Nyāya-Vaiśeṣika admits the concept of *khaṇḍakāla*, especially the threefold division of time as speech-dependent. We take it as real as our ordinary language demands such a measurable time.

As far as the notion of Time, including the threefold division of time, is concerned one may note certain similarities between Nyāya-Vaiśeṣika and Bhartṛhari. Both accept that Time as an eternal, all-pervading principle. Both admit that the phenomenal world cannot be explained without the concept of Time. But for Nyāya-Vaiśeṣika, Time is one of the substances assumed to explain the nature of the empirical reality. Along with Time, earth, water, air, fire, etc. are accredited with equal status. But they are of the form of corporeal atom. But Time, ether, space and soul are incorporeal, though all of them come under the category of substance. In their realistic and atomistic scheme of metaphysics though Time plays an important role, it is not the sole principle responsible for the change and experience of the reality. Time is the common or formal cause of the non-eternal substances. Bhartṛhari, on the other hand, conceives Time as a creative power. So far as we are in ignorance (*avidyā*) about the true nature of the reality, the idea of Time as well as its powers – *pratibandha, abhyanujñā, karma, jarā, bhūta, bhaviṣyat* and *vartamāna* – are meaningful. But all such functions have relevance as long as our knowledge and experience are limited to the empirical world. The moment the true knowledge dawns, the entire universe is realized as appearance. Thus Time is the first creation of the appearance.[9]

It is of some interest to note that Bhartṛhari disagrees with the Vaiśeṣika notion of threefold division of Time. He thinks that the Vaiśeṣika notion of threefold division of Time is inconsistent with its doctrine as according to their theory a thing is non-existent before its production as well after the destruction. But the object we encounter in the world is characterized by sequence. It is the nature of the way we describe the reality of the objects. According to Bhartṛhari, as long as we are talking about the phenomenal reality in terms of time we must take it to be a series of activities (*kriyā-vivartta*) rather than the object (*mūrti*). In this context he makes it clear that the activities are divided in terms of time and the material forms or objects are divided with reference to space.[10] Moreover the division of time in relation to an activity is continuous. The activity of cooking is anticipated the moment the pot is put on the fire, thus we can say *pacati* (is cooking). Similarly, we can say *apakṣit* (he has cooked) as soon as some moments of the activity are past. Here the activity of the past is taken into consideration. Again, taking into consideration the future

---

9 *Vṛtti* on III.9.62.

10 III.7.153.

moments of the same activity, one can say *pakṣayati* (he will cook).[11] Thus all the three states of time are taken into consideration when we talk about activities. As time is the dividing factor of activities, an activity is verbally treated as something to be accomplished; and as possessing sequence. This makes the usage of all the three tenses possible.[12] Therefore the definition of activity and also the usage of different tenses are only verbal not real.

However, Nyāya-Vaiśeṣika finds its staunchest critic in Śrīharṣa who challenge its notion of threefold division of time. But I would like to gloss over the details as my chief concern is to look at the Nyāya-Vaiśeṣika model of time from the standpoint of Bhartṛhari. So rather I would like to shift my focus to another interesting dimension of the debate about the nature of past, present and future that we come across in Nyāya literature, especially of Gautama and Vātsyāyana. This I would deal with a little later.

Yoga and Buddhist on the Division of Time

YOGA

The Buddhists as well as the Yoga system of philosophy do not admit the reality of time as an independent principle. Yet they cannot deny that our speech is marked by the division of time. Our language expresses the events and facts of the world in terms of past, present and future. But according to their metaphysical scheme no event or fact could be delimited in terms of time as everything is a process; the only reality is the series of incomprehensible moments. So how can one talk of the threefold division of time? Let us now observe what the Yoga system has to say about such usages as past, present and future. The *Yoga-Bhāṣya* on *Yoga-Sūtra* 3.13 has the following view on record:

---

[11] III.8.5.

[12] III.8.1.

> Just as the atom is the minimal limit of matter, so the moment is the minimal limit of time, or the time taken by an atom in motion in order to leave one point and reach the next point is a moment. But the continuous flow of these is sequences (*krama*). Moments and the sequences of these cannot be combined into a real (*vastu*). Thus, time, being of this nature, does not correspond to anything real, but is a product of mind, and follows as a result of perception of words.[13]

The idea of a continuous and singular time as well as the division of time in terms of past, present and future are finally word-dependent (*śabda jñānānupati*). We do not have in reality any such chunks of time as past, present and future as reflected in our day-to-day language. Thus the significance of threefold divisions of time remains meaningful within the limits of language (words) not in the sphere of reality.

One may note that there seems no apparent difference between the Nyāya-Vaiśeṣika view and the Yoga view (as well as the view of Bhartṛhari) as far as the unreality of the division of time is concerned. All these views finally refer to the way our language functions. But the real difference lies with the ontological framework within which a system of thought works. According to Vyāsa the commentator of *Yoga-Sūtra*, the moment is objective and rests on the sequences (*kṣaṇas tu vastupālitaḥ kramāvalambī*). The sequence is essentially an uninterrupted succession of moments which is called *kāla* by experts. Logically speaking, if two moments cannot occur simultaneously, then it is impossible that there be a sequence of events that occur simultaneously. When the later moments succeed an earlier there is the sequence. Since in the present there is the single moment, there are no earlier or later moments. Therefore there is no combination of them. But those

13 *sa khalva ayam kālo vastuśūnyo 'pi buddhinirmāṇa śabda jñānānupāti* – *Yoga Bhāṣya*, quoted in P.S. Sharma, 1972, p. 22.

moments which are called past and future can only be explained as inherent in the changes (*pariṇāma*). But according to Yoga, the world passes through change in a single moment; so all the external aspects of the world are related to the present moment. Thus the present becomes the only state that can be experienced not the past and the future. Yet in certain sense the Yoga system does not dismiss the importance of the past and future. According to it the substance continues to exist though its external form varies. So in the states of the objects of the world there is bound to be mutation in the form of the time-form. The past cannot be totally severed from the present and future.

SAUTRĀNTRIKA BUDDHISM

We have discussed in the previous chapter how the Sautrāntrika Buddhism with an alternative metaphysical scheme tries to dismiss the reality of the one and indivisible Time. According to them the phenomenal world is characterized by series of moments. So what is ultimately real is the moment. These moments are characterized as point-instants (*svalakṣaṇa*s). They can be perceived but cannot be conceived. For, the act concept formation involves putting the experienced characteristics under a class or universal. Being the product of the mental faculty such universals do not have any reality since the moments alone are real. So the names or forms we ascribe to our experiences of the objects and actions of the world are but convenient fictions of our mind (*kalpanā* or *vikalpa*). Accordingly, Yogācāra had denied the reality of the time – be it eternal or non-eternal – for *svalakṣaṇa*s do not have any duration. Thus we note that though there is some unanimity of opinion among the orthodox Yoga school and the non-orthodox Yogācāra Buddhism so far as the unreality of the time is concerned (since both of them conceive time as a mental construct) yet their ontological scheme varies widely from one another. According to Yoga, *aṇu*s (elemental moments) are substances that actually exist, while for the Yogācāra school of thought *svalakṣaṇa*s or the moments are not substances. Yet, as far as our knowledge of the threefold division of time is concerned both can only admit the reality of the present since it is perceivable though not conceivable. Thus Sautrāntrika–Yogācāra negates the reality of the past and the future. The only real is the dynamical moment of the efficacious activity (*arthakriyākāritva*). This is essentially the present, though in this case present is not understood in the ordinary sense of the term. However, they finally admit that we can as well use such words as past, present and future in our linguistic exchange or while describing the experience. But they all are finally mental constructs.

The Relative Priority of Past, Present and Future

STATUS OF THE PRESENT

From our discussion so far, it follows that for most of the philosophical systems these three terms – past, present and future – seem to emerge more out of the compulsion of our ordinary linguistic usage, rather than the metaphysical obligation. But as I stated earlier, Indian philosophical systems could not overlook the importance of the linguistic issues related to our study of time as a concept. So our philosophical tradition, depending on its respective ontological perspective, offers interesting arguments about the relative priority of past, present and future. In our day-to-day life we notice that we can be more sure of the present rather than the past or future. Past is deposited in the memory and future is something that has not yet arrived but anticipated. So "present" seems to be in a better position to be ascertained. Most philosophical systems of India that admit the reality of time as a principle, too, admit that the present belongs to a separate category than the past and future. Yet the concept of present is not as uncomplicated as it appears to be. The points that need attention are – as time seems always to move ahead what should be the criterion of our categorizing the present? Is it the present that endures for a moment or should it be understood as an action that has started and not yet completed? Again, if it is a moment as Yoga and Sautrāntrika–Yogācāra would make us believe, then can we have a glimpse of the present? In this section I would like to focus on such debates regarding the status of the present-time.

Present as Unreal

I would like to begin with the view that denies the reality to the present while admitting the reality of the past and future. In *Nyāya-Sūtra,* we come across such a fascinating debate over the issue. In this case Gautama, the author of *Nyāya-Sūtra,* defends the theory of threefold division of time against his (imaginary) opponent who admits the significance of the past and future but refuses to admit the relevance of assuming the present.

Gautama in his *Nyāya-Sūtra*[14] develops his theory of the threefold time in the background of the opponent's (*pūrvapakṣa*) view that the "present" has no reality, since it is not essential for understanding the past and future. So it is not necessary to admit the existence of the present in addition to the two others. Here the *sūtra* does not identify the opponent. So we are not sure which system of thought holds such a view. May be such a view was prevalent during his time; or *pūrvapakṣa* is imagined so that the proponent's thesis could be logically scrutinized. The opponent who argues against the necessity of assuming the present time might give the example of a falling body. Let us spatially represent the path by a line. We can then identify a particular point in the line and say the falling body has already traversed it. This length may be taken to correspond to what is called the past. But we

[14] *Nyāya-Sūtra* 2.1.39-43.

also notice the other stretch of the line which the falling body is still to traverse. Since this has not already been traversed in the past this will have to be traversed in the future. Therefore, the time the falling body will require to traverse is divided into two parts, namely, the past and the future. It thus leaves no room for the present.

Gautama and Vātsyāyana reject the contention of the opponents by simply pointing out that this is simply a spatial illustration. A spatial line can be conceived to be divisible into two parts without leaving any remainder. But this picture cannot be true of time. On this ground it is not justifiable to hold that time consists only of the past and future without the present intervening between the two. Vātsyāyana points out that the distinctive character of time can be understood best by reference to *kriyā*. If there was no present time, then there would be neither the past nor future, as both of them depend on the notion of present.[15] When the action of falling down stops that is called past, when the action of falling down continues it is the present; and when the action of falling down of the object will be produced this is called the future. If the opponent does not cognize the action of falling down as going on, then with reference to what he can say that the action of falling down has ceased or going to be stopped. So the other two times are dependent on the act of falling down which is the state of the present. In other words, the term past is used when the connection of the object with the act of falling down has ceased. The word future is used when the connection between the object with the action is still to come. In both the cases, the "action of falling down" determines the concept of the past and future. So it is the action which is "present". So it is the action which manifests time not the spatial position.[16]

15 *Nyāya-Sūtra* II.1.40.

16 *Nyāya vārttika*.

Moreover, the present time is the indicator of the existence of objects. So we use such expressions as "a substance exists", "an attribute exists". In this case "exists" denotes the present time. So Gautama says:

> In the absence of present time nothing is cognized, as no perception is possible.[17]

Gautama and Vātsyāyana, therefore, conclude their defence of the concept of the present by the following epistemological argument. According to them knowledge is of different varieties. Non-perceptual knowledge is basically distinct from perception. But it is nevertheless dependent on perception in some way or the other. Perception always refers to such things that necessarily exists. If something is not existent, there cannot be any perception of it. Theoretically speaking, the past thing could be an object of past perception or the future thing may be an object of future perception. But perception testifies the existence of its object at the time of perception. Thus, there is a correlation between the time of perception and the time of existence of its object. We are constantly in possession of perception of this or that object. If we are not unduly skeptical and accept the possibility of knowledge and of perception, the present is very much real. It has in it the stamp of difference from the past and also the future. Again, Gautama argues that there can be three types of *anumāṇa* (inferences); in two of which we proceed either from the perception of the effect to the existence of the antecedent or from the existence of the antecedent to the consequent. For example, by looking at the wet ground we infer that there had been a rainfall; or in the reverse way, from the perception of gathering of clouds in the sky one infers that there will be rain soon. In both the cases the relationship, that is our basis of inference, is temporal in nature. So the knowledge of the past and future is dependent

---

[17] *Nyāya-Sūtra* II.1.43.

on inference. Vātsyāyana developing this idea further argues that inference as a source of knowledge leads us to the knowledge of only facts of the past or future. But perception as a source of knowledge is restricted only to the realm of the present. As inference is ultimately based on perceptual knowledge we cannot dismiss the status of the "present".

According to Nyāya-Vaiśeṣika, perception is due to the sense–object contact. Therefore, that which is not present cannot be in contact with the sense-organ. If we go by the opponent's standpoint then there is nothing called present and consequently nothing called existent. This would mean that the opponent dismisses the validity of perception as such, including the cause of perception, the object of perception and the cognition through perception. Thus if perception is denied, all other proofs of right cognition are also denied. This would finally imply that the opponent practically deny everything of this universe.[18]

Interestingly, Bhartṛhari too argues almost in similar lines against his opponents who deny the reality of the "present" in the 85-89th *kārikā*s of Kālasamuddeśa. As in the case of *Nyāya-Sūtra*, here too he does not disclose the identity of the exponents of the theory of non-reality of the "present". In this case we are also at a loss to know to whom Bhartṛhari is actually referring to. Some scholars like P.S. Sharma are of the opinion that it is the Mādhyamika view. But as it would be obvious from the following discussion the opponent could not have been the Mādhyamika Buddhists, who deny the reality of time in any form. The *kārikā*s clearly indicate how the reality of the present time is challenged. I quote two from such *kārikā*s.

> A thing either is or is not. There is no third possibility. Therefore, excepting past and future, there is no middle course. – 85

[18] *Nyāya-Bhāṣya* II.1.43.

> A thing, being free from distinctions, cannot be in the nature of sequence. How can one thing, whether be it existent or be it non-existent, be in the nature of sequence? – 86

Now let me elaborate the opponent's argument. An action is a process or series of moments. The moment that is past is something which has been accomplished. As far as the moment that is coming is concerned, the action is still in future. There cannot be a moment that is both, past and future, existent and non-existent at the same time. So there cannot be a "present" moment. That which "is" cannot have sequence; and that which "is not", too cannot have a sequence. There is no third category. Therefore there cannot anything be called "action" consisting of sequence, so there cannot be a "present" occurring in sequence. The opponent further argues that we also cannot say that a large number of moments arranged in a sequence is action; and that it would be called present till the production of the accomplished goal, because the moments cannot be simultaneous. Only one of them can be perceived at a time. Nor can we perceive a sequence. So the opponent's position is as follows, that in the different moments, there is some common feature, which is action. Action would then thus be a common feature existing at each moment and not a unity of series of moments. So we cannot call any action as referring to the present time.

Bhartṛhari refutes the opponent's view with a totally different way of defining the "present". He says:

> When perceived in its own form, that is, that which enables it to produce fruit, that is the present time. – 89

According to Bhartṛhari, action is one – a unification of moments. Rather a sequence of moments having one purpose is called action. It is one because it has one purpose. In his Kriyāsamuddeśa of the third canto of the *Vākyapadīya* he defines action as:

> Whenever something finished or unfinished is presented as something to be accomplished, it is called "action" because of its having assumed the form of sequence.[19]

Actions vary with purposes. Even if some moments are present and some moments are absent, an action can be said to be "present". The present should be defined as *prārabdhapari-samāptatvam* (a fact of having been begun but not yet finished). A sequence of moments, all leading to the same result, if looked upon as one, even before the result is produced, can be said to be present.[20]

Bhartṛhari's conception of the "present" seems to be largely influenced by Patañjali's *Mahābhāṣya*. There is elaborate discussion on the status of the present in this great work. Patañjali, the Bhāṣyakāra on Pāṇini's *Aṣṭādhyāyī* sums up the case for the "present" in the following way:

> The present does exist. It is not perceived like the motion of the sun. Yet it is there. The five lotus fibres in the inside of the lotus-stalk when being burnt are not noticed as being burnt, similarly subtle things are knowable only by inference. We use *gacchati* (he goes), for there is action which is present. How? First, there is a mental action, the desire to achieve something. This mental action leads to physical action. Both these actions, mental and physical, prior and posterior, ending with the production of the fruit, are unified by the mind which has the power of piecing things together and presented as one action. The use of the present tense *gacchati* is therefore perfectly justified.[21]

Present only Real

In case of Buddhism we come across some contradictory yet interesting views on the notion of threefold time division of

19 *VP* III.8.1.

20 Iyer 1965: 64-65.

21 *Mahābhāṣya* on Pāṇini 3.2.123.

time. Though most of the schools admit the original Buddhist conception of *anitya,* there seems to be no unanimity regarding the nature of the reality of time. Similarly, one comes to notice divergent views regarding the status of the past, present and future. In *Abhidharmadīpa-vibhāsaprabhāvṛtti* we come across a description of four schools within Buddhism regarding the status of the past, present and future. Kāśyapīyas (close to Sthaviravāda) hold that present alone is real. For them, the past that has borne fruit cease to exist; and the future which has yet to ripen does not exist. So present alone exists. Vibhajyavādins, a form Sthaviravādins, also deny the existence of the future and also of the past that has borne fruit.

But the most powerful argument regarding the status of present comes from Vasubandhu and Diṅnāga. Both of them reject the Buddhist Vaibhāsika theory that the threefold division of time is valid.

In this context it would be of some interest to note the Vaibhāsika versus Sautrāntrika face-off regarding the reality of past, present and future as recorded in the Buddhist treatise *Abhidharmakoṣa-Bhāṣya.* The Vaibhāsika argues that the proof of the three divisions of time lies in the fact that consciousness is the result of the two factors – its organ and content. A mental consciousness, for instance, arises in regard to an object only when the object is already past, because it belongs to the previous moment. A factor can only arise with an existing object as its content. If past and future factors did not exist, then there would be factors without objects. If past did not exist how could good and bad actions give their retributions? For when the retribution arises the actions are already past. When a factor exercises its function it is present, when it does not exercise its function it is future. When it has exercised the function and has stopped, it is the past.

Vasubandhu challenging this argument states that if a factor exists always, then why does not it always exercise its function?

If its functioning ceases why not the object itself? To this query Vaibhāsika explains that a conditioned object which has not arisen itself is called the future; one having arisen but not having destroyed is present; one which has been destroyed is the past.

Sautrāntrika argues back that if one believes that *all* exist, how they be taken as not yet arisen (future) or is already destroyed (past)? But Vaibhāsika believes that the essential nature of the object continues to exist. Still the question may be raised that – how can one talk about arising at all if everything exists all the time? So Vasubandhu concludes that past is that which existed, the future is that which will exist. In this sense they exist, but they do not exist in the way the present exists. As to the argument that past and future exist because consciousness arises as the result of the past and future events, one may ask – are these events really generative conditions of objects? A future event, which may arise in thousand years, or which may never arise may be the object of consciousness. So it is very difficult to see how it can be the generative factor of a present event? Something that does not exist can very well be an object of consciousness, such as when we are conscious of fancies. Thus on this ground it would be wrong to assume the existence of the three times – past, present and future.[22]

Further, Sautrāntrikas argue:

> Some say past and future exist and define existence as the content of awareness. But many things can be content of awareness that does not exist. Past and future do not exist for they have no function or efficacy; so they do not exist. If a thing has no function, it has no self-nature (*svalakṣaṇa*). All factors arise from cause and condition. Since past and future have no causes and no conditions they do not exist. If

22 *Abhidharmakoṣabhāṣya, Encyclopedia of Indian Philosophies,* vol. VIII, pp. 554-57.

> the future exists then things would have to be eternal and non-created. So only the present is real.[23]

But it must be made clear here that the Sautrāntrika–Yogācāra conception of the present cannot be taken in the sense in which other systems of thought talk of the validity of the present. Here the present refers to the perception of point-instants that, though have causal efficiency, is not experienced as duration.

So we notice that within Buddhism itself there are some schools which admit the validity of past, present and future, while some others reject the validity of the present admitting only the past and future. Again, there are schools of thought like Sautrānrika–Yogācāra which only admit the significance of the present.

Past, Present and Future with Same Status

Most of the schools of the classical systems of Indian philosophy, including Yoga which advocates time as atomic; and some schools of Buddhism and Bhartṛhari admit the relevance of the threefold division of time.

One of the most prominent schools of Buddhism, viz. Sarvāstivādins, staunchly support the idea that threefold division of time is real and past, present and future have the same status. According them the individual and the universe are subject to constant change in their external aspect (not in essential nature), the past determining the present condition, and the present the future. There is no need for postulating the changeless being in ourselves: for the unbroken continuity of the present with the past, or of the future with the present, would assure us that there is no loss of identity. Thus this school of thought admits the reality of the threefold division of time. Schayer very rightly observes:

---

23 *Abhidharmakoṣabhāṣya, Encyclopedia of Indian Philosophies,* vol. VIII, pp. 554-57.

> The [Satvāstivāda] doctrine of Traikālyavāda is an interesting and original attempt at replacing the hypostasis of substantial Time by another hypostasis, viz. that of real future and past elements of being.[24]

Interestingly, the Yoga system too admits the validity of *trikāla* (three divisions of time). We have seen that this system defines time in terms of the infinitesimal atom. The time required by an atom to move its own measure of space is called a *kṣaṇa* which really hooks to the present. Hence time as "duration" is a construction of mind (*buddhi-nirmāṇa*). So it may appear surprising that how the Yoga system accommodates the notion of the threefold time. Yoga justifies the idea on the ground of the notion of change. Atoms, according it, are continually changing places. So at each moment the universe is undergoing change. The collocation of atoms at one moment is different from what it was in previous moment. This change of the moment leads to change in the every object of the universe. This change can be seen as past, present and future. When any change is in potential state we call it a future; when manifested, it is present; when it becomes latent, we call it past.

Past, Present, Future as Unreal

We come across another alternative view in Buddhism that demolishes all the claims regarding the division of time in terms of past, present and future. This view is reflected in the philosophy of the Mādhyamikas. They argue that the three time-distinctions are made on the basis of relation of one to the other. Time division of the present and future is made on the basis of the past. But in what sense are they dependent? The time-divisions are never there all at once. When one is present the other two are absent. On the one hand if they are present at the same point of time they would be indistinguishable from one another; on the other hand if it is

---

24 Schayer 1991: 310.

argued that these three are not relative to one another, the question crops up – what serves as the basis of such division? A non-relative past, present or future is inconceivable. In other words to infer the existence of time on the basis of the usage of division of time is untenable. Thus the division of time on the basis of past, present and future has no real basis. According to Mādhyamikas:

> Time is nothing more than temporality in terms past, present and future at conventional level. This means that even from the empirical point of view time is not a reality, and temporality of sequence of events (or entities) shows their relational origination and thus voidness their own nature *(niḥsvabhāvatā/śūnyatā)* from the ultimate point of view.[25]

Advaita Vedānta, too, dismisses the reality of both Time and *khaṇḍakāla*. According to Śaṅkara temporality is a relative term that has some validity in the empirical world. But the absolute Reality defies logic and language. So it is beyond the modes of speech, including names and forms. Since the phenomenal reality has no ontological status, time too is not an independent reality. Śaṅkara in his commentary on the *Vedānta-Sūtra* says that time is an effect of *avidyā*.[26] It makes *kāla* objective in the sense in which effects of *avidyā* are, viz. they are not the constructions of the human mind. Time has relevance for phenomenal world, i.e. an appearance of the *Brahman*. But, according to Advaita Vedānta, the source of time and time consciousness is akin to apperception which "is not something different from the I-am. *The present then of time is the presence of the aspect of I-am in apperception*, which collects together past and future into the present. This collecting is done by the memory and anticipation."[27] This way of time consciousness

---

25 Prasad 1991: xiv.

26 *etena dik-kāla-manoḥ-paramānvādinām kāryatvam vyākhyātām* – II.3.7

27 Raju 1985: 427.

in terms of past, present and future, is not a mental construct but is a mental event. It is based on the subjective states of remembering, perceiving and anticipating. The subject who experiences it has the subjective consciousness of "I am" through which these states are interrelated. If the three states of time are mental or may be psychological then temporal events are phenomenal events. According to Prasad,[28] this psychological reduction of time in Advaita serves the useful purpose, transcending the temporal and realizing the timeless. According to Advaita all *sādhanā* is in time. Apart from a general condition of spiritual perfection, time can be employed as an object of meditation. It has been a general impression that Advaita Vedānta and Mādhyamikas dismiss time as a phenomenon. But a close look at their metaphysical position reveals that the concept is too important to be ignored totally.

Our discussion on *khaṇḍakāla* reveals that as long as we are talking about the human life, his experience, thought and his expression of thought about the world, the crucial issue of division of time into past, present and future have to be acknowledged. The difference in interpreting the subject though lies in the preferred ontological structure from which it is viewed.

---

28 Prasad 1991: 9.

7

Time and Creation

So far we have examined the two dimensions of Time, viz. *akhaṇḍakāla* and *khaṇḍakāla*, from Bhartṛhari's standpoint, keeping in the backdrop the two other models – time as substance and time as atom expounded by Nyāya-Vaiśeṣika and Buddhism–Yoga, respectively. In this chapter I would like to examine the concept of time from the standpoint of philosophical cosmology. This discussion carries a lot of importance in view of the fact that the question of time has relevance only with reference to the empirical world that is characterized by change, sequence and progress. Indian philosophers who admit the reality of time have always been obsessed with exploring the relation between the Reality (that is most often taken as eternal and unchanging) and the empirical world that is sequential and mutable in nature. Such an explication would be impossible without reference to the notion of time directly or indirectly. Though the scientist may take such deliberations as speculative, philosopher's attempt to understand the nuances of the concept of time in relation to cosmology cannot be just dismissed as a futile attempt. Keeping this discussion in the backdrop I would like to throw some light on how Bhartṛhari, as a philosopher of language, handles the issue.

Cosmogony is one of the topics in which Indian philosophy, religious scriptures and literature have taken a lot of interest. So we come across varied theories about the creation of the universe. We cannot dismiss all of them as a speculative non-sense; for some of these speculations are backed by logic. Philosophical cosmogony in Indian tradition, as opposed the scientific cosmology, holds that even if there is creation it is not in time. No Indian philosophical cosmogony would admit that the world was created at a particular moment in time. It is not somebody's command – "Let there be the world and there was world". It is a process of evolution or may be manifestation. Both Bhartṛhari and Nyāya-Vaiśeṣika who grant the reality to time find good reasons to talk of time in two senses – in the transcendental sense and in the empirical sense. What unites the two senses is that the word time signifies certain magnitude. Like spatial magnitude or extension, temporal magnitude or duration also characterizes things. This is the principle that exists whenever a thing is said to exist. But Time in the absolute sense is said to have infinite magnitude (*vibhu parimāṇa*). In empirical level it is seen as principle that stands related to substance that has motion. The temporal distinctions like younger or older, subsequent or simultaneous bear reference to time (*kāla*). The principle of time is that to which reference has to be made whenever we assign any measurable temporal duration to any substance. But this measurable time is different from the Time that is not measurable in terms of finite magnitude. To take a metaphor from Bhartṛhari Time is like a weighing machine that weighs everything but it itself is not measurable. There is no circularity here because the Time itself is not a temporal duration. Further this magnitude is infinite, though this does not mean infinite duration. Infinitude has been so defined so that it does not make any reference to duration. Time's infinity is not a measurable quantity involving addition of moments of time. So Time is conceived as eternal (*nitya*).

In this context it will be of some use to understand what the Indian philosophical tradition means by the word "eternal". The word may signify "everlasting" or else "transcending time". Both the senses imply that it is not possible that there could be a time preceding or succeeding it. This means that eternal thing has a non-temporal sense. Thus if the world is created it is not created at a particular point of time. That which is created in time cannot be eternal. So creation means coming in contact with a time that was already there. In the cosmological sense Time has all along been there; it is not created with the creation of the universe.

Causality and Time

In Indian tradition, especially in cosmology a distinction is made between causality and the ultimate principle. Though God/*Śabda-Brahman/Brahman/Prakṛti* are regarded as the efficient cause and sometimes as the material cause, the tradition uses the word cause in a quite distinct sense. Cause and effect relation, if admitted, is operative in a phenomenal sense. Such causal relation is operative among the objects and events that are related in terms of precedent and consequent. God/*Brahman/Prakṛti* cannot be the cause of the phenomenal world in this sense. Yet most of the systems of thought discuss about the evolution of the world in terms of material or efficient cause. Bhartṛhari too holds that *Śabda-Brahman* is the material cause of the world. What do they mean by such a claim? Does the philosopher like Bhartṛhari mean that the *Śabda-Brahman* transforms itself to the phenomenal world? Or else do they mean that it is the changeless background of the phenomenal world? To understand its dimensions let us have a cursory look at some of the theories prevalent in the Indian philosophical system about the nature of the process of transformation and manifestation. There are five well-known doctrines in this regard.

1. The doctrine of beginning or construction (Ārambha-vāda).

2. The doctrine of combination (Saṁghātavāda)
3. The doctrine of real change (Pariṇāmavāda)
4. The doctrine of appearance (Vivarttavāda)
5. The doctrine of reflexion (Ābhāsavāda).

According to Nyāya-Vaiśeṣika the phenomenal objects are due to the conglomeration of the atoms (*paramāṇu*s), which are regarded as indivisible units. The changes in the objects as well as the production of the objects are due to the coming together or disintegration of these atoms. So the atoms are the material cause of the world. When a number of atoms combine together they produce a gross object; and when they disintegrate the result is the destruction of that object. The process of integration and disintegration goes on endlessly. In the initial phase the atoms are in a state of vibratory motion which results in the combination of two at a time that is called dyad (*dvyāṇuka*). While in combination the atoms do not merge their individuality. So the wholes are as real as the parts. But in their opinion the manifested world of objects is not potentially present in the atoms. Each combination of the atoms brings about a new beginning (*ārambha*).

According to the Sautrāntrika and the Vaibhāsika schools of Buddhism an effect is nothing more than the aggregate of the *kṣaṇa*s. But these units of reality are mutually exclusive and there cannot be any physical connection among them. Unlike Nyāya it believes that the physical connection is a fiction if it is to be understood in abstraction from the objects that are said to be connected. The combination of atoms results in the conception of objects (*saṁghāta*). So it may be categorized as Saṁghātavāda.

According to Pariṇāmavāda when a cause undergoes change it turns into an effect. The effect is potentially there in the cause. The milk turning into curd is often given as an example to illustrate this standpoint. Like the milk being manifested as the curd, the phenomenal world is the manifestation of the potential Reality. So the manifestation is real as the Reality is conceived as its potential womb. Sāṁkhya philosophy is one of the chief exponents of this theory. According to it, the material cause of the world is the primordial matter (*prakṛti*). It may be noted that the Yoga system of philosophy as well as the Vaiṣṇava Vedānta schools of thought like Madhvas and Nimbārkas subscribe to this account of the evolution of the phenomenal world. Here the primordial Reality is the material potentiality that transforms into the world. Hence the objects and events of the world share the characteristic reality of the potential state. The phenomenal world is *pariṇāma* (real effect) of the cause that exists in the form of the Reality.

The Vivarttavāda, on the other hand, holds that the phenomenal world is not the real transformation but a case of superimposition like the cognition of truth as untruth. Śaṅkara, the exponent of the Vivarttavāda, holds that the realty that we ascribe to the phenomenal world is due *avidyā* (nescience). The phenomenal world in fact is an appearance (*vivartta*) of the Reality.

The Trika philosophers of Kashmir neither accept Pariṇāmavāda nor Vivarttavāda. According to them Consciousness (*caitanya*) is the only Reality. This is all-embracing and all that we experience lies within it. Thus what is usually called as external is held to be a reflection of the consciousness as there is reflection on the mirror the individual self as the original is reflected in the mirror (*ābhāsa*). The manifestation of the universe is due to unrestricted freedom of Consciousness and is a process of reflection. This is labeled as Ābhāsavāda. According to this school of thought the phenomenal world is an appearance (*vivartta*) due to *avidyā*. It is as much real as an image is real.

Bhartṛhari: Vivarttavādin or Pariṇāmavādin?

In the background of these five general theories of cosmogony let us now examine Bhartṛhari's position on this issue. We have seen that Bhartṛhari uses the word *vivartta* quite frequently with reference to the relation between *Śabda-Brahman* and the world. There were at least two opinions about the philosophy of *Śabda-Brahman* in relation to the evolution – one explaining it in terms of Pariṇāmavāda and other in terms of Vivarttavāda, as is obvious from Vācaspati Miśra's *Nyāyakaṇikā*, Jayanta Bhaṭṭa's *Nyāyamañjarī* and Śāntarakṣita's *Tattvasaṁgraha*. In the face of such conflicting opinions it is quite difficult to place Bhartṛhari's true position. Interestingly, he has indiscriminately used both the terms – *vivartta* and *pariṇāma* – in connection with the evolution of the phenomenal world from the *Śabdatattva-Brahman*.[1] It appears to us that Bhartṛhari was not familiar with the connotation of the two terms that acquired significance in the post-Śaṅkara period. But even in case of Śaṅkara the term *vivartta* is sometimes used to convey an import which is expressed by the term *pariṇāma*. He used the term *vivartta* to explain the Sāṁkhya view of evolution.[2] So we may find no connotational difference between the two terms in the works of Bhartṛhari. But in the post-Śaṅkara phase when these two terms acquired definite connotations there were attempts by the commentators of Bhartṛhari's *Vākyapadīya* to place him in proper perspective. The grammarians like Bhaṭṭojidīkṣita feel that Bhartṛhari could not have accepted the Pariṇāmavāda theory. Not only Bhaṭṭojidīkṣita but the commentators like Helārāja and

---

1 *sabdasya pariṇāmo 'yam iti āmnāyavido viduḥ* ।
chandobhya eva prathamam evam viśvamvyavartata ॥
– *VP* I.121

Again, *vivartate arthabhāven prakriyā jagato yatah* । – I.1

2 *Śārīrakabhāṣya*, Commentary on *Brahma-Sūtra*, Nirnaya Sagar Press, 1917, p. 488.

Puṇyarāja share this opinion. This is well known that Bhartṛhari adheres to Advaitism as is evident from the very first *kārikā* of *Vākyapadīya*. In this famous *kārikā* itself he uses the word *vivartta* to explicate the notion of the One and ultimate reality – *Śabda-Brahman* – revealing/appearing in the form of plurality of the world. In his *vṛtti* on this *kārikā* he defines *vivartta* as "the assumption by the One, without losing its Oneness, through apparent diversity, of separate unreal forms".[3] This offers credence to the view that Bhartṛhari shares a form of Vivarttavāda. Many interpreters feel that Bhartṛhari is the precursor of Śaṅkara as far as a philosophy of non-dualism (Advaita) is concerned.

The Connotation of Vivartta for Bhartṛhari: Differing Interpretations

Before we assess Bhartṛhari's position let us have a look at the implications of the word *vivartta* as brought out by Jayanta Bhaṭṭa.[4] According to him the term could have as many as four implications. First, *vivartta* means material change. So by implication *Śabda-Brahman* changes into the phenomenal world as milk changes into curd. Second, *vivartta* may mean unreal representation. So the phenomenal world is unreal. Third, *vivartta* may mean formal transformation which means *Śabda-Brahman* assumes the forms of the objects as the rope assumes the form of snake. According to the fourth implication of the term *vivartta*, *Śabda-Brahman* is the creative principle of the world. As I have stated earlier, most of his commentators go for the second implication of the term. Since Bhartṛhari offers a theory of non-dualism his commentators like Puṇyarāja and Helārāja read into his theory the form of non-dualism presented by Śaṅkara. Puṇyarāja identifies the Bhartṛharian

3 *ekasyā tattvadapracyutasya bhedānukareṇasatyavibhaktānya-rūpagrahītā vivartah* – quoted in Iyer 1969: 449.

4 *Nyāyamañjarī* II.103-04.

notion of *Kālaśakti* with the Śaṅkara's notion of *avidyā*. In his opinion *Kālaśakti* is neither real nor unreal, hence false. He also interprets *vivartta* as connoting appearance. Absolute does not change its own nature in the process of evolution. But it was Helārāja who convincingly interpreted Bhartṛhari's theory of cosmogony in terms of Śaṅkara's non-dualism. He was so sure about the similarity between Śaṅkara's non-dualism and Bhartṛhari's non-dualism that he takes the word *avidyā* as used by Bhartṛhari to mean the power of *Śabda-Brahman*, viz. *avidyāśakti*. It must be noted that Bhartṛhari talks of *vidyā* and *avidyā* but he does not clearly state whether *avidyā* is the power of *Śabda-Brahman* or not (*VP* II.233). But Helārāja speaks of *avidyāśakti* as the nescience with the dual function, viz. that conceals the real nature of *Brahman* as well as the principle that projects the one *Brahman* as the multiplicity of forms before the individual soul. The difference between *avidyā* and *Kālaśakti* lies in the fact that the former conceals the true nature of the reality and exhibits the plurality of the phenomenal world; the latter presents the phenomena in temporal order.[5] Thus the phenomenal world is an appearance superimposed upon the foundational reality of *Śabda-Brahman* through the operation of *avidyā* which is seen as the root of multiplicity and difference; and *Kālaśakti* is the ground of projecting the non-sequential as sequential. These two principles though existing from eternity are ultimately as false as the phenomenal world is their product.

Among the modern scholars, Pt. Gaurinath Sastri likes to differ with the interpretation offered by Puṇyarāja and Helārāja. As Bhartṛhari nowhere explicitly mentions about Vivarttavāda in Śaṅkarite sense he feels that we cannot take his use of the word *vivartta* at the face value implying that the

---

5 *akrame brahmāṇi bhedavabhāsanāmavidyā kṛtam* ।
tatriva kramābhāsanaṁ kālākhya-svātantrya śakti kṛtam ॥
– quoted from Iyer 1969: 446

world is an appearance. However K.A.S. Iyer supports the *vivartta* thesis on the ground that *avidyā*, as mentioned by Bhartṛhari, is not ordinary ignorance but a metaphysical ignorance. On the other hand, M. Beardeau argues on the basis of the original *kārikā*s of *Vākyapadīya* that there is no justification about holding that the phenomenal world that emerges out of *Śabda-Brahman* as unreal. Beardeau comes to the conclusion that

> the phenomena do not veil the Being but reveal it, or rather, the Being manifests itself through them. It is logically necessary for the system to postulate the Being as pure unity and non-differentiation in order to explain the profound correlation of the objective and subjective aspects of reality. But it is more pertinent for its proper content to postulate the Being to be the Word. The Being is not One and then many in course of its evolution. Nor is it One really and then many phenomenally. . . . One is therefore, justified in saying that the ontological reality holds within itself the phenomenal diversity, but the phenomenal diversity is the only thing to which we have access, because it is the only thing we need and which really interests us. Thus one understands why it would be inconceivable to look for and, *a fortiori*, to find in *avidyā*, metaphysical ignorance and *māyā* (cosmic illusion) which forms the pivot of the Vedāntic thought.[6]

Before we evaluate Bhartṛhari's position in this context let us have a re-look at his conception of *Śabda* – as the Reality Supreme. According to him one of the characteristics of *Śabda-Brahman* is its omnipotence.[7] While elucidating the line "from whom the creation of the world proceeds", the commentary says:

---

[6] Quoted Iyer 1969: 131.

[7] *sarveśvaras sarvaśakti – Puṇyarāja's Commentary on Vākyapadīya*, Benares Series, p. 51.

> . . . the universe proceeds out of the *Brahman* which is of the nature of Word, devoid of all inner sequence; from that involution (*saṁvṛtta*) in which all diversity has merged and is undifferentiated and is inexpressible, all transformations being in *latent* stage.[8] [Italics mine]

For all practical purposes its unlimited power to manifest is discernible in the field of the cosmos. The point can be illustrated through the following example provided in commentary of the Brahmakāṇḍa of *Vākyapadīya*:

> As at the end of the summer the rainy season collects mass of dark cloud that finally over-pours in the form of rain, similarly *Śabda-Brahman* by means of the *Kālaśakti* makes it possible for the so-called causal powers to produce objects of various descriptions.[9]

Thus this character of the omnipotence of *Śabda-Brahman* enables us to comprehend its character as an agent by virtue of which it initiates the process of evolution of the phenomenal world. It acts as the living dynamic force. It stands as the regulating principle of all phenomenal acts. This omnipotence of *Śabda-Brahman* implies that it is also the efficient cause of the world. At the same time it is also the material cause of the phenomenal world. So it is omniform and omnipresent. It is the unchanging matrix of the manifold changes. It is conceived as the one seed of all that sprouts into multiplicities of the phenomenal world.[10] It is the centre from which radiates infinite variety of objects that are experienced, the beings that

---

8 *Vṛtti* on *VP* I.1 (tr. Iyer).

9 *Vākyapadīya*, ed. Carudeva Sastri, 1934.
prakṛtitvam api prāptān vikārān ākaroti saḥ ।
ṛtudhāme va grīṣmānte mahato megha samplāvan ॥ – Sastri 1934: 9

10 *ekasya sarvavijasya yasya ce 'yam ankadhā* ।
bhoktṛbhktavyarūpeṇa bhogarūpeṇa ca sthitiḥ ॥ – *VP* I.4

experience and the process of experience itself.[11] So *Śabda-Brahman* is conceived to be present in every object. So we may come to the conclusion that Bhartṛhari means by *vivartta* not just appearance but some sort of latency.

Bhartṛhari and Śaṅkara on Vivartta

Now we seem to stand at crossroads. The problem arises because philosophers and scholars seem to have a fascination for fitting Bhartṛhari in the mould of a more famous and more widely accepted Advaitism of Śaṅkara. So let us have some idea about what Śaṅkara has to say on the issue. While delineating his conception of *Brahman* he writes in his *Bhāṣya* on Bādarāyaṇa's *Brahma-Sūtra*:

> That omniscient and omnipotent source must be *Brahman from which occurs the birth, continuance and dissolution of the universe that is manifested through name and form, that is associated with diverse agents and experiences, that provides the support for actions and results, having well-regulated space, time, and causation, and that defy all thoughts about the real nature of its creation.*[12]

We must first of all note that as far as the nature of the empirical world is concerned, he does not differ much from Bhartṛhari. The world is not unreal in the sense of an illusion. Here appearance is not without some reality, though of a secondary order. But at the same time Śaṅkara would not like to go into the question of how the phenomenal world is related to *Brahman*; for he says "it defies all thoughts about the real nature of creation". In other words it is inexplicable. The relation could at best be understood in terms of *adhyāsa* (which has been translated as superimposition). Śaṅkara defines *adhyāsa* as "the appearance of a thing where it is not". It is attributing

---

11 *VP* I.4.

12 Gambhirananda 1977: 14.

to real, that is non-dual, a world of duality and plurality. In this context it may be noted that for Śaṅkara, time is just an element of the phenomenal world that is characterized by name, form. The process of birth, death and continuation of the universe is attributed to *Brahman*.

Keeping Śaṅkara's idea of the relation between the highest Reality *Brahman* and the phenomenal world in the background, let us assess Bhartṛhari's position. First and foremost, we must not ignore the fact that his brand of Advaitism is different from Śaṅkara's Advaitism. This has been amply justified. In his case *Brahman* is of the nature of *Śabdatattva*, the *eternal verbum*. So he is not primarily concerned with the reality or the unreality of the phenomenal world. The phenomenal world that the individual cognizes is determined by the nature of the Word-essence. So the world is word-determined. But he has no compulsion to explain, what actually is the nature of the world? The world may exist ad infinitum, but it finally depends on how we cognize and experience the objects of the phenomenal world and express them through words. All that we express about the objects is but *vikalpa* – a mental construct. We cannot catch in the web of language all the aspects of an object. The world of objects for Bhartṛhari is nothing but how do we express the conception of the world through our language. As all our cognitions are possible through conceptualization or *vikalpa*, it necessarily involves selection and elimination. We only cognize some or other aspect of the object as presented to the finite mind. So we can experience only a part of the reality. A word like *ghaṭa* cannot express the whole of what a jar stands for. It can only express a part of it, viz. "jarness". If one wants to refer to the colour of the jar then he has to use another word and another universal for it, viz. "redness".

The incompleteness of our cognition comes within the range of our knowledge either through sense or words expressed, with some limiting factors, such as universal. Our cognition is always vitiated by *upādhi*. So a word is incapable of expressing the whole of an object. Thus, all the three – the object, its cognition and the word expressive of it – are all tainted with limitedness. This explanation again points to the fact that Bhartṛhari does not hold that the phenomenal world is just an appearance. He highlights that the reality of the phenomenal world is ungraspable. The original being/existence (*mukhyasattā*) remains ever elusive. The individual can only cognize the secondary/metaphorical existence of the phenomenal existence. For Bhartṛhari unity and indivisibility only are true and real (*vidyā*). Anything that is divisible, differentiated and presented in bits and pieces has lesser degree of reality. So we may conclude that according to Bhartṛhari the phenomenal world as grasped by us, that has only a secondary existence, is appearance.

To understand Bhartṛhari's position vis-à-vis the process of evolution of the world from *Śabda-Brahman* we must make it clear that Bhartṛhari did not subscribe to any theory of causation. I have discussed in Chapter 3 how Bhartṛhari dismisses both – Satkāryavāda and Asatkāryavāda (Pariṇāmavāda or Ārambhavāda). He rather holds that by a miraculous course of action the sequenceless *Brahman* is transformed into sequential world process. Still the question remains – does the phenomenal world evolve out of *Śabda-Brahman*? As I have stated earlier he is not very explicit on the issue. We may guess that *Śabda-Brahman* is taken to be the material cause in the sense that every object is determined by the verbal form. An object which is determined by a word cannot be confused with another object which in turn is determined by another verbal expression. An object is understood by the verbal expression signifying it. This very conception of evolution needs the concept of time, as the word-determined thought and existence characterized by change and multiplicity. This explains why Bhartṛhari brings in the notion of *śakti* (*Kālaśakti*) with reference to *Brahman*. Obviously, the notion is logically needed to relate it to the phenomenal world which is not static but a process. Power (*śakti*) in this case implies the potency of *Śabda-Brahman*. The potency and the Reality cannot be seen as two independent entities. So instead of saying that the relation between *Brahman* and the phenomenal world is inexplicable, he conceives the phenomenal world in terms of it language-determined nature that may be said to be rooted in the Word-essence or *eternal verbum*. The unity of the Word-essence expresses itself through the limitations of human intellect in terms of multiplicity in the level of experience. But the Ultimate Reality, viz. *Śabda-Brahman,* is inexplicable and ineffable and it is not language-determined. Human language cannot be used without differentiation and discrimination. Language is based on concept formation and categorization through names. All such processes involve limitation through determination. So though Bhartṛhari subscribes to a form of Vivarttavāda, it is different from Śaṅkara's theory. For Bhartṛhari *Śabda-Brahman* is the Ultimate Reality because it is undifferentiated, One and unitary, but the phenomenal world though is characterized by differentiation, plurality and diversity; and hence is attributed as metaphysically non-real, its nature is not completely cut off from its source. If we go by Jayanta Bhaṭṭa's categorization then in case of Bhartṛhari *vivartta* may signify that *Śabda-Brahman* is a creative principle that is closely linked to the phenomenal world.

I have already stated in the chapter on Śabdādvaitavāda that, as a non-dualist, Bhartṛhari's challenge rests on how to link unity with the multiplicity and non-changeability with changeability. I have discussed therein how at every level of linguistic expressibility we move from diversity to unity. For example, words (sound patterns) and meaning merge to express the sense that is intended to be communicated. Again the difference between the speech and thought is merged to make the intention of the speaker and the understanding of the hearer possible. Finally, he elaborately shows how our diversified speech (*vaikharī*) points to a pre-verbal stage in the level of our thought (*madhyamā*); and this further points to a state of non-verbality (*paśyantī*). Here there is neither sequence nor diversity observed in the other two levels, viz. *vaikharī* and *madhyamā*. But the immense potentiality of the human beings to express their thought, experience, imagination, in brief, the entire range of the power of verbal expression, remains as the seed. It is an undifferentiated unity. So throughout his analysis of philosophy of language Bhartṛhari's emphasis is on the intricate relation between unity and diversity. But in his opinion more the unity, more the principle real. So he meticulously exhibits how there is a tendency of diversity to move towards unity; and finally to a point of unity. Again the principle of unity has a latency to as if to burst forth (*sputṭ*) into diversity. Therefore while explicating Bhartṛhari's position regarding his views on creation one should not and cannot ignore the fact that he is primarily a philosopher of language. It is the very concept of language that provides anchorage to his non-dualistic metaphysics.

Time and Causality in the Phenomenal Level

To put the views of Bhartṛhari regarding the causal power as it operates in the phenomenal world it may be stated in brief that Time is the creator of the cycles. It holds back the various functions of everything and then releases them so that the potentialities come to mature at the appropriate time as particular manifestations of eternal activities. Then the power called inheritance (*samavāya*) sublates differences and gives rise to an identity, as it were, between effects and their causes. This identity is prompted by universal, which come to be reflected in the particular effect. Then the qualities (*guṇa*), conditioned by their own causes, come to be perceived in those effects and in turn lead to the manifestation of their own universals. Because the locus of the particulars is eternal, they persist over a period of time dependent on relevant causes of sustenance, and continue to perform their functions with the help of other existing things. Eventually Time, through its power called "decomposition" (*jarā*), which is opposed to its other powers called *krama* (sequence), prevents things from performing their functions by developing propensities that are contrary to those functions, which in turn results in the conjunctive elements of the object disintegrating. So the thing perishes.

According to Bhartṛhari casual powers operate through two aspects of *Kālaśakti*, viz. *krama* and *jarā*. Thus when *Kālaśakti* permits causal powers to operate it is revealed in the aspect of *krama*. So every object comes into being through different sequences of time. When the same *Kāla* is seen from the aspect of decay and decimation, it is called *jarā*. So the causes not only bring about the effects, but also the cessation of those effects. But the most vital fact about Bhartṛhari's notion of *Kālaśakti* is that he conceives the phenomenal events as sequential due to the two powers of *Kāla* – *abhyanujñā* and *pratibandha*. The question of sequence relates primarily to action and next to phenomena appearing and disappearing thereof. As *Kālaśakti* governs all actions and presents them in sequence it is natural to expect that the attributes of succession is ideally associated with it. But in final analysis *Kālaśakti* is neither affected by the sequence nor by actions that constitute the nature of the phenomenal world.

Thus far, we have been discussing the question of the relation between time and creation in the context of philosophical cosmology. Philosophical cosmology, that formed an important part of the Indian philosophical tradition, does not use the word *kāraṇa* (cause) in the phenomenal sense. Most of the systems of thought believe that the cause–effect relationship in the phenomenal level is possible only when all other conditions are fulfilled. So the creation of the world is not sudden but absolute. There is divergence of opinion regarding the nature of Ultimate Reality; and also regarding the nature of the transformation or manifestation in the form of the phenomenal world. Despite such divergences it is believed that time is closely associated with change as well as cause. Bhartṛhari in this respect makes it clear that time is the phenomenon that initiates change, not only in the phenomenal level but in the level of the manifestation of the One and sequenceless *Śabda-Brahman* in the sequential and plural universe. Bhartṛhari's theory of creation is therefore closely linked to his conception of *Kālaśakti*, without which his metaphysical positions remain unexplained. Here the Reality as *Śabda-Brahman* stands for the principle of potentiality that embraces within its womb the diversities as well as change.

8

Kālaśakti, Māyā, Avidyā and Śabda-Brahman

BHARTṚHARI's Kālasamuddeśa can be said to be a unique piece of literature that reflects on the varied nuances of the concept of time. So far I have attempted to throw some light on this Nyāya-breaking work in the backdrop of other philosophical systems, especially, Nyāya-Vaiśeṣika, Buddhism, Yoga and Advaita Vedānta. I would like to wind up the discussion by focusing on some concepts that are likely to create confusion in the proper assessment of this work. The two concepts that particularly attract the attention of the scholars are the use of the word *śakti* with reference to *kāla* (time) and the word *avidyā*. Unless these two issues are properly analysed it may appear that Bhartṛhari lacks logical coherence and the philosophical rigour.

Kālaśakti and Māyā

As we have noted in the previous chapter, the traditional (Helārāja) as well as the modern scholars (Iyer, Sastri and others) find it fascinating to put Bhartṛhari's philosophical viewpoints within the mould of Śaṅkara's Advaitism. It is seldom realized that Bhartṛhari preceded Śaṅkara at least by two centuries. Bhartṛhari adheres to the Upaniṣadic concept of *Brahman* as the highest metaphysical principle; and very much in the line of the Upaniṣads he conceives this Reality to be non-dual One, inexpressible, supreme consciousness. This non-dual Reality for Bhartṛhari is *Śabdatattva*. But the Advaitin tenor in his thought is not enough to guarantee that Bhartṛhari did not have his own variety of metaphysics. This has been discussed in some detail earlier too. But what needs some more attention at this juncture is the apparent similarity between Śaṅkara's conception of *māyā* and Bhartṛhari's idea of *Kālaśakti*.

To examine how close Bhartṛhari's philosophy is to Śaṅkara's Advaita philosophy one must have a quick look at some of the basic concepts of these two forms of Advaitism. We find that Śaṅkara and Bhartṛhari offer a similar account of the highest Reality called *Brahman*, though for the latter *Brahman* is of the nature of the *śabdatattva*. Both agree that this Reality is non-dual, defies all descriptions as it is beyond the categories of thought and language. Both agree that though ineffable *Brahman* is not a pure abstract principle but the material cause (*upādāna kāraṇa*) and efficient cause (*nimitta kāraṇa*) of the empirical world, which is characterized by diversity and plurality (and also change). Finally, both, Bhartṛhari and Śaṅkara agree that the diversities (change?) we notice in the conception of universe would be impossible without a cause which is absolutely perfect and self-sufficient. This self-caused cause is *Brahman*, which expresses itself through the multiplicity of universe. The phenomenal world, though has practical and empirical reality, has a secondary status; hence from the metaphysical standpoint unreal and untrue.

But the most crucial question that any non-dualist has to face is: how to explain the relation between the two levels? How the One and unique could be the cause of the phenomenal world of diversity? In case of Śaṅkara, he introduces the concept, viz. *māyā/avidyā* to explain this ticklish issue. *Māyā* according to him is not only ignorance but positive wrong knowledge. It finitizes the infinite and makes the unlimited appear as limited *jīvas*. It also produces the false notion of plurality and difference. According to Radhakrishnan, Śaṅkara introduces the concept of *māyā* because the world is not self-explanatory hence the problem of the inconceivability of its relation to *Brahman* could be explained only in terms of *māyā*. *Māyā* is principle which accounts for *Brahman* as the world. Bhartṛhari instead introduces the notion of *Kālaśakti* to explain the relation between the undifferentiated *Brahman* and the differentiated level of the phenomenal world. But do these two concepts, viz. *māyā* and *Kālaśakti* have the same ontological function?

In case of Bhartṛhari *Kāla* is the driving power inherent in *Śabda-Brahman* which is the first cause of the bursting forth of the worldly phenomena. Though some of the schools of Advaita, like Vivaraṇa school, locate *māyā* in the *Brahman*, it does not attribute to the *māyā* the "driving force" as one of its characteristic. We find that two dimensions are attributed to *māyā* – obscuring (*āvaraṇa*) and projecting (*vikṣepa*), more stress is laid on the later aspect rather than the former. So it becomes alluring for the scholars and interpreters to compare *māyā* with *Kālaśakti*. For Bhartṛhari, *Kālaśakti* is a power that projects (*vikṣepa*) the undifferentiated into differentiated phenomena of the world. But we must remember that *Kālaśakti* not only projects but it is also attributed with "driving force" that is associated with "action". This difference is not only the difference of word but the difference has also an important ontological implication. For Śaṅkara, the projected world of *māyā* is neither real nor unreal but a case of superimposition (*adhyāsa*); but Bhartṛhari has no need for introducing *adhyāsa* as an element involved in the explication of the relation between the *Brahman* and the *jagat*. For him the "Time" that projects the phenomenal world, though transcendentally unreal, never loses its ontological identity with *Śabda-Brahman* as its *śakti*. The illustrations offered in *Vākyapadīya* are more associated with *Śabda-Brahman* as illumination (*sphoṭa*) and potency. This is evident from the metaphors he uses. For example he compares the ultimate form unity as peacock egg that has all the colours of a fully grown-up peacock with colourful plumes, potentially present within it. "The energy (*kratu*) called the Word existing within, as the yolk in peacocks egg, has an action-like function and assumes the sequence of its parts."[1] Similarly he compares *Kāla* with the driving force like pushing-up or lifting-up of the water-wheel (*kālayati*). Such illustrations demonstrate that Bhartṛhari had to offer a different type of non-dualistic ontological scheme totally distinct from Śaṅkara's ontological scheme.

If we have a deeper look at Bhartṛhari's non-dualism we cannot overlook that some of the basic tenets of Bhartṛhari's philosophy do not fit in well with Śaṅkara's Advaitism. If the philosophy of Bhartṛhari is interpreted in the light of Śaṅkara's Advaita then it does not do justice to his unique notion of *Kālaśakti*. I have explained earlier that *Kālaśakti* serves as the basic link between the diversity of the phenomenal world and the uniqueness of *Brahman*, which in no way disturbs his non-dualism. But Śaṅkara would never admit of the reality of any power coexisting with the Absolute. If Bhartṛhari's position is to be equated with Śaṅkara, then the very concept of *śakti* must be declared as meaningless.

Before we make further comments on Bhartṛhari's Advaitism let us have a re-look at his theory of *Śabda-Brahman*. It may be guessed that by describing *Śabda-Brahman* as identical in essence with *Kālaśakti* (which is designated as the *svātantrya śakti*) he wants to emphasize that the unrestricted agenthood forms the very essence of the Supreme Reality. Bhartṛhari views the Supreme Reality just not as the locus or the passive background for the play of the power but as the power itself.

[1] *VP* I.51.

This is why he talks of *kratu* in the verse quoted above. Freedom to act is one of the characters of *Śabda-Brahman*. In the metaphysical scheme of Śaṅkara such power to manifest is explained with reference to the concept of *māyā*. But *māyā* is never the essence of *Brahman*. So *Brahman* is an action-less substratum on which *māyā* plays the role. But *māyā* is neither identical nor distinct from *Brahman*. Consequently, it is held to be as a false adjunct. So the conceptual status of *māyā* largely remains unexplained.

Again, in case of Śaṅkara the primary concern is how to explain the relation between the unity of *Brahman* and the diversity of the phenomenal world. But the focal point seems to be the element of "multiplicity"; and not the phenomenon called "change". But in case of Bhartṛhari "multiplicity" and "change" both seem to get equal attention. To highlight on the aspect of "change" he conceives *Śabda-Brahman* also as *akrama* (non-sequential) in contrast with the sequentiality and activities of the phenomenal world (*jagato prakriyā*). Hence, his concept of *Kālaśakti* cannot be put under the straightjacket of the Advaitic conception of *māyā*.

Despite the status Śaṅkara's Advaitism enjoyed and continue to enjoy in the intellectual world one cannot fail to notice certain amount of conceptual discomfort in relating the transcendental level of *Brahman* and the phenomenal level of the *jagat*. The concept of *māyā* is too amorphous to explain how the two radically opposed levels are linked. But Bhartṛhari rather connects the two levels by conceiving the highest Reality (*Brahman*) as of the nature of the *Śabdatattva*. As he portrays every phenomenal activity including thought, awareness, cognition as well as the process of the world constituted of objects and events as *word-determined*, it becomes easier for him to relate the phenomenal with the transcendental. Besides, Time as an inherent aspect of the highest Reality helps Bhartṛhari to show that the time-driven world may not be as real in metaphysical sense but it never loses its contact with the highest Reality (*Śabda-Brahman*).

> The relation between the phenomenal world and the *Brahman* for Bhartṛhari is continuous and does not have the mysterious break of an "all or nothing" sort that *māyā* doctrine and its rope–snake analogy requires.[2]

Bhartṛhari does not need to take recourse to the idea of *adhyāsa* or superimposition. If Bhartṛhari accepts time as the power of *Śabda-Brahman*, which is independent of all beings; and at the same time driving them to act in a sequential manner, the world cannot be a case of *adhyāsa*. Śaṅkara brings in the notion of *adhyāsa* to claim that the plurality is superimposed upon the passive *Brahman*. So the concept of *māyā* that remains unexplained without the concept of *adhyāsa* does not fit in with the Advaitism of Bhartṛhari.

Avidyā, Kāla and Śabda-Brahman

From our discussion so far this is evident that Bhartṛhari uses the concept of *Kāla* as a *śakti* to explain the relation between the Word-essence and the world. But along with this he brings in a second concept that he thinks, is necessary for his Śabdādvaitism. So in Brahmakāṇḍa of *Vākyapadīya* he not only introduces the notion of *Kālaśakti* but also another important concept, viz. *avidyā*.[3] He uses the concept also in the 62nd *kārikā* of Kālasamuddeśa wherein he states:

> It (Time) is first to be manifested in the state of *avidyā* and it does not exist in the state of true knowledge (*vidyā*).[4]

---

[2] Coward and Raja 1990: 40.

[3] *VP* I.1.

[4] *saktyātmadevatāpakṣaibhinnam kālasya darśanam* ।
prathamaṁ tadavidayāyām yad vidyāyām na vartate ॥
– *VP* III.9.64

Let us now gather some idea about how this term *avidyā* is used in the philosophy of Bhartṛhari. Does the term imply the sense in which it is usually translated, viz. nescience, or does it signify something profound? The pair of terms *vidyā* and *avidyā* has been often used in the epistemological sense in the Indian philosophical tradition. In the Sāṁkhya and Yoga system *avidyā* means the absence of true knowledge of the qualitative difference between *Puruṣa* and *Prakṛti*. In the Vaiśeṣika, *avidyā* stands for the absence of the knowledge of *padārtha* which constitutes the real ontological and epistemological elements of the universe. In Advaita Vedānta the term *avidyā* is inherently linked to *māyā*. *Avidyā* could be interpreted as the absence of the true knowledge of the identity between the *ātman* and *Brahman*. According to all these systems of thought overcoming *avidyā* and obtaining *vidyā* leads to *kaivalya*, *apavarga* or *mokṣa*. Now let us examine how Bhartṛhari uses the concept in his philosophy. The term occurs twice in his *Vākyapadīya* (*kārikās* II.233 and III.9.62). In both the cases the word *avidyā* appears along with the word *vidyā*. In second canto (233) he states that all the differentiations in the level of communicative speech and the science of grammar are due to *avidyā*. Transcending the differentiation and subsequent realization of the unity and oneness of the *Śabda* is *vidyā*. So it seems that for Bhartṛhari *avidyā* rather signifies the element of differentiation rather than nescience. We may come to the same conclusion if we have a close look at Helārāja's commentary on the 62nd *kārikā* of Kālasamuddeśa:

> The power [*śakti*] called *avidyā* is responsible for the One becoming many, for the emergence of the phenomenal world. The diversity is both temporal and spatial. The former comes first. The power called Time is responsible for appearing in temporal sequence.[5] Consciousness at the first stage is called

[5] Iyer 1969: 124.

> *paśyantī*, is without sequence. When it becomes associated with the *prāṇa* principle (activity), it shines as Time, as though it had sequence. The reality called *Brahman* is without any sequence and consists of true knowledge, and it is not affected by time.[6] Under the influence nescience (*avidyā*) it appears as this and that. Thus through the intervention of Time the phenomena appear in a temporal sequence to the individual selves coming down from the time immemorial. *Because all differences consists of nescience* all divisions of Time, from different points of view, are also the creation of nescience. Once true knowledge dawns, all differentiations disappear and, therefore, the division of Time disappears. Therefore, to discuss whether this (the division) is right or not, would result in labour only. In empirical stage everything is unreal and the truth cannot be determined. This is the substance of what is meant.[7] [Italics mine]

We note that here Helārāja attaches the word *śakti* to *avidyā*. So calls it *avidyāśakti*. But it may not be taken to be something novel conceived by Helārāja. In the *vṛtti* of the first *kārikā* too Bhartṛhari uses the word *śakti* with reference to *avidyā*, where it is stated that the diversity of "the static (*mūrti*) and dynamic (*kriyā*) is due to the activities of the *avidyāśakti*" (*mūrtikriyāvivartau avidyāśaktipravṛttimātram*). It appears from the *vṛtti*s I.1-2 that that the word *avidya* was used, in this sense, even in earlier texts as is evident from certain quotations used by him. In one of the old quotations found in the *vṛtti* it is stated that all phenomena in the form of concrete objects (*mūrti*) and actions are only the functioning of the power of *avidyā* that can be said to neither identical nor different from the true knowledge.[8] In another verse quotation, equally

---

6 Quoted from Iyer 1969: 123.

7 *ata evaitat kāladarśanam . . . tattvāvyavasthānupapatterityatra tātparyārtha* – III.64.I.23, tr. Iyer, quoted from Iyer 1969: 545-46.

8 *VP* I.1-3.

untraced, it is stated that *Brahman* transcends change and mutability but is soiled by *avidyā*; hence manifests itself as differentiated. In both the quotations *avidyā* is seen as projecting the One and changeless Reality as having many forms arranged in spatial and temporal sequence.[9] It is the principle of multiplicity, and change, but the multiplicity and transience have lesser reality than the One and undifferentiated *Brahman*. So we cannot wish away the importance of the concept of *avidyā* in Bhartr̥hari's philosophy. The nature of the relation between *vidyā* and *avidyā*

> seem to be rooted in the paradoxical coexistence of two principles in the world – unity and diversity – are represented on the one hand, by the unity of *Brahman* and multiplicity of things, on the other, by the unity of meaning and multiplicity of means (phoneme, word-forms, etc.) which manifest it. . . .[10]

Now let us find out how the two crucial concepts – *Kālaśakti* and *avidyā* – may be connected. Helārāja's commentary on the 62nd *kārikā* of Kālasamuddeśa, quoted above, makes it clear that in his opinion the main function of *Kālaśakti* is to present the phenomena in temporal sequence. So in his cosmology Bhartr̥hari offers priority to the emergence of the temporal order. At the same time he talks of *avidyā* also. The ultimate reality is One and without sequence. But it has also infinite powers. So the cosmos emerges out of it with all the multiplicities. But the multiplicity is in temporal order. So *avidyā*, as a principle is perceived to be the cause of the One appearing as many in the form of the phenomenal world (*saṁsāra*). Again Bhartr̥hari talks of *prāṇa*. Here *prāṇa* is

---

9 *tadetadamr̥tam brahm nirvikārāmavidyāyā* ।
kaluṣṭvamivāpanna vedarūpam vivartate ॥
– *VP* I.1-2. Quoted from Iyer 1969: 448

10 Ivanov 2009: 257-58.

understood as the activity, an inner urge to manifest and to set things in motion. So we find that *Kālaśakti* is connected on the one hand with *avidyā*, and on the other with activity. This is why Helārāja brings in the notion of *avidyā* quite frequently in his commentary on Kālasamuddeśa. According to him the individual self/the seer has limitations due to *avidyā*. Therefore the individual self is the part of the phenomenal world. While explaining the statement of Bhartṛhari that the undifferentiated (*avikalpita*) as differentiated assumes multiple forms, he speaks about the distinct roles of *avidyā* and *Kālaśakti* in the manifestation of the cosmos consisting of *mūrti-vivartta* and *kriyā-vivartta*. Helārāja also says that it is due to *avidyā* coming down from the eternity. The universe which is manifested under its influence consists, first of all, of infinite number of experiencer (*bhoktā*), who is really identical with the Reality being of the nature of the consciousness. They experience the universe which like them is an emanation of *Śabda-Brahman*. The universe consists of infinite number of constantly changing and constantly inter-acting objects. This is due to *Kālaśakti*. It must however be made clear that Bhartṛhari at no stage identifies *Kālaśakti* with *avidyā*. *Avidyā* has distinct role to play. Helārāja frankly admits about the distinct functions of the *avidyā* and *Kālaśakti*:

> The former brings about *differentiation in the undifferentiated Brahman* and the latter is responsible for the *temporal sequence in which the differentiated phenomena* are presented to the individual perceiver.[11] [Italics mine]

Helārāja in his commentary highlights on another role of *avidyā*. It not only brings about differentiation but also limitation. The individual self which experiences the objects is limited in

---

[11] *akrame brahmāṇi bhedavabhāsanāmavidyākṛtam* ।
tatraiva kramābhāsanam kālākhya-svātantryaśakti kṛtam ॥
– quoted from Iyer 1969

its cognition but also in its power to act.[12] On account of limitations we are not able to cognize an object as it is.

We have tried to justify that in the ontological level *avidyā* is the cause of multiplicity and differentiation in the principle of unity. But in the linguistic level too he uses the term *avidyā* with the same implication. This is evident from Bhartṛhari's use of the word *avidyā* in another context.[13] In the second canto that primarily deals with the nature of sentence and sentence-meaning, he states that all the differentiations described in grammar, consisting of various ways of analysing sentences into roots, stems, prefixes and suffixes, are unreal in the final sense. It is a case of the artificial division of the One and the indivisible. When ultimately the true knowledge (*vidyā*) dawns one realizes that the Word-principle is but indivisible.

The Phenomenal World and Change

As I have stated earlier that from Bhartṛhari's *kārikā* and Helārāja's *vṛtti* it appears that the concept of "multiplicity" of the phenomenal level of existence is as important as the concept of "change". According to Bhartṛhari change means the infinite number of processes, actions and states through which they pass all the time. They all can be brought under the sixfold transformations of being like, birth, etc. The changes being actions and processes take place in time or the temporal sequence. Here the power called Time plays its role. These processes and changes are collectively called *kriyāvivartta* which is controlled by *Kālaśakti*. Changes presuppose things which undergo changes. They are the concrete objects (*mūrti-vivartta*) that is the product of the previous processes and actions and now involved other processes and actions. But they are different from the processes and actions. Such objects too have

12 *VP* III.1.8-9.

13 *VP* II.233.

a sequence, but arranged in spatial order or *dik* (direction or position). They have the potentiality to change and undergo different processes. In this sense they are the means (*sādhana*) for the accomplishment of certain temporal states. What is called the means is not the object itself but their potentiality, though they cannot be separated. Though their capacities/ potentialities are infinite the science of language identifies them as six *kāraka*s. Here the implication is very clear. Though Bhartṛhari seems to talk of *Kāla* in a metaphysical sense it has to be finally understood in terms of how we describe and talk about the phenomenal world. All these objects which is distinct from the process or action are called *siddha* – the finished or the accomplished state – as distinct from actions or events which are in the process of being brought about; and therefore called *sādhya*. Explaining Bhartṛhari's position K.A.S. Iyer very lucidly analyses the relation:

> From one point of view then, the universe consists of two kinds of things: *siddha* and *sādhya*. *Siddha* objects are arranged in spatial sequence and collectively called *mūrtivivartta*. The processes and actions, which are *sādhya*s, are collectively called *kriyāvivartta*. To say that the universe consists of *siddha* and *sādhya* is equal to saying that it consists of *mūrtivivartta* and *kriyā-vivartta*, manifested under the influence of *Dikśakti* and *Kālaśakti*.[14]

Now it is mandatory for us to solve a crucial issue. Is the world manifested by *Śabdatattva* through its powers like *Kāla* and the principle like *avidyā* are essentially unreal? We have noted that if we follow Helārāja then we have to admit that *avidyā* is not only ontologically superfluous, but it stands for the metaphysical ignorance.

---

[14] Iyer 1969: 126.

Bhartṛhari and Advaitism: The Semantic and Ontological Perspectives

We have already noted that there are certain distinctively different strains in the Advaitism of Śaṅkara and Bhartṛhari. Despite the leanings of the commentators like Puṇyarāja and Helārāja; and also some modern scholars like Iyer[15] and Gaurinath Sastri[16] the relation between *Śabdatattva-Brahman* and the phenomenal world cannot be and should not be understood in the light of Advaita Vedānta. If we admit this standpoint then *avidyā* comes to play a more vital role than *Kālaśakti* that has been so clearly highlighted in the Brahma-Kāṇḍa of the *Vākyapadīya*. So one may also view the issue from the standpoint offered by Kunjunni Raja and Harold Coward according to whom we may infer that there are three ontological levels in Bhartṛhari's thought – *Brahman*, his powers of space and time, and the diversity of the phenomenal world. This is something quite contrasting to Śaṅkara's notion where there is one ontological level, viz. *Brahman* – with *māyā* as an epistemological second level (which is neither real nor unreal but inexplicable). For Bhartṛhari the highest ontological level is pure *Śabda-Brahman* without sequence or diversity. It is the culmination of our knowledge of the *vāc* or language principle (*Śabda-Brahman*). Although Time is inherent in *Śabda-Brahman* at this stage, no sequence has occurred. It is the pure potentiality. The next ontological level, in descending order is *madhyamā*. At this stage the Time drives *Śabda-Brahman* in sequence with the help of *prāṇavṛtti*. Our experience of language in this stage corresponds to the diversification of the unitary *sphoṭa* into the mental sequence of thoughts. The full-blown appearance of diversity appears when Time has released all secondary cause–effect relations that have been stored in the

15 Iyer 1969.

16 Sastri 1959.

memory traces (*saṁskāra*) and the seed of expressibility (*śabda-bīja*). It is in this third (*vaikharī*) level that the power of Time as found in the ordinary cause–effect relation is fully experienced by the individual self. Time is thus the governing power of all activities of the manifested objects. It is the Time that drives objects into action to the point at which their secondary cause–effect relations take the hold. But it is also behind the scene activity of Time that controls the extent of the secondary action of objects, along with their moment of decay or withdrawal.[17]

This is more than clear that Bhartṛhari's ontological position is largely determined by his position as a philosopher of language. He finds an inextricable relation between the language and Reality. This claim could be strengthened by the fact that following his predecessor Patañjali he too makes it clear that he is more interested in explicating his philosophical position in terms of the way language works rather than contemplating on the nature of the phenomenal reality. This may be one of the reasons why he identifies the Reality supreme as *Śabdatattva-Brahman*, rather than *Brahman*. Here the principle of language or *eternal verbum* serves as the final anchor. Had his position been so close to Śaṅkara he would not have been so severely criticized by Śaṅkara himself.

At the same time Bhartṛhari was not a mere grammarian (Vaiyākaraṇika), he was a philosopher (Dārśanika) too. He was a non-compromising non-dualist. So for him the Ultimate Reality is One and indivisible. We can steer clear of the apparent controversies regarding the use of the term *avidyā* if we also care to note the fact that his ontology and linguistic analysis almost run parallel. This stand can also be evidenced by the fact that he deals with the principle of language at three levels – metaphysical, semantic and grammatical. In the ontological level he discusses language as *Śabdatattva-Brahman*;

---

17 Coward and Raja 1990: 41.

in the semantic level he discusses language as it is used in linguistic communication (*lokavyavahāra*); in the grammatical level he analyses language into grammatical parts like roots, suffixes, etc. (*śāstra-vyavahāra*). Bhartṛhari explicitly admits that from the absolute standpoint the language in use (dealing with word, meaning, sentence, intention of the speaker, hearer's understanding, etc.) are secondary or artificial. There can be no difference between the word and meaning, speaker's intention and hearer's understanding, for all divisions are unreal and they finally lead to unity. Similarly, he admits that the grammatical analysis into different parts of speech, etc. is artificial. This grammatical analysis is undertaken so that we can proceed from division to unity. Thus both, the semantic analysis and grammatical analysis are due to ignorance (*avidyā*) about the real nature of the principle of speech. But such analysis is undertaken to arrive at the true understanding of the nature of reality that is One, indivisible and inexplicable. As we have discussed so far, Bhartṛhari advocates that unity or non-duality is truth (*vidyā*) and the diversity and divisibility are untruth (*avidyā*). But the reality becomes a cipher unless it is connected with the plurality of the world that the individual encounters. So if anyone has to realize the ultimate reality he has to pass from the untruth to truth, from *avidyā* to *vidyā*. The phenomenal world to which we have access is conditioned by change and diversity. At the same time this world that is given to us is language-determined. However, before we come to the final analysis of true significance of *Kālaśakti* in ontological, semantic and syntactical level we must throw some light on Bhartṛhari's notion of Time and action.

Time and Action

According to Bhartṛhari the phenomenal world consists of particular objects (*mūrti-vivartta*) and actions (*kriyā-vivartta*). In this case also his notion of Time and action can be enunciated from two angles – ontological and linguistic. I would prefer to start with the former. To understand the basic relationship between the concepts of *Kāla* and action from the ontolgical standpoint let us have a close look at the 12th *kārikā* of Kālasamuddeśa:

> *pratyavastham tu kālasya vyāpāro 'tra vyavasthitaḥ* ।
> *kāla evāhi viśvātmā vyāpāra iti kathyate* ॥

> Here (in this world) at every stage, certainly the operation of time is established. For, indeed activity is called time, the soul of the universe itself.

The above *kārikā* clearly establishes that though the world is thought to be constituted of objects (*mūrti-vivartta*) it is a dead and lifeless world without activity. Perhaps no metaphysical system would like to delineate the phenomenal world as conglomeration of relatively static objects. For example, in Nyāya-Vaiśeṣika the objects are a distinct category (*padārtha*) along with action as a separate category. Buddhism which does not admit the reality of time as an entity does not face the problem of relating the time and action. For them the world is an endless process of series of moments. But once the reality of time is admitted the relation between the time and action needs explication. The *kārikā* quoted above throws some light on Bhartṛhari's way of looking at the two concepts – *Kāla* and action. He admits that the world is characterized by change and sequence. This is also evidenced by the fact that in the introductory verse itself he talks of *jagato prakriyā,* i.e. the processes of the world, not simply *jagat*. The world signifies a process for him. So all the objects come into existence continue to exist and in due course perish due to time. These processes finally refer to the activities. All the activities of the beings are due to the power called time. Hence time is identified as the "soul" of the universe. The world that we experience is seen as a "process". The phenomenal world is not series of moments but a series of sequences that makes the "order" as well as the change possible. Things are not just meaningless flow of moments. Nor the series of moments are directionless. So the conception of time is closely associated with action. We find an echo of the same idea in the 34th *kārikā* of Kālasamuddeśa:

> The manifestation of the All-inclusive principle, as though with a sequence and as though with parts has been said to be action.

Commenting on this stanza Helārāja says:

> *Brahman* is beyond all diversity and differentiations, has all the power within it and can manifest itself in all forms. Under the influence of the *svātantrya śakti* called *Kāla*, it presents itself in a sequence and that is action.

Correspondingly, while defining action Bhartṛhari says:

> Whenever something finished or unfinished, is presented as something to be accomplished, it is called "action", because of its having assumed the form of sequence.[18]

Elucidating it further he says:

> What is called action is a collection of parts produced in a sequence and mentally conceived as one and identical with parts which are subordinate to it.[19]

Helārāja commenting on this *kārikā* says:

> The moments or parts come into existence to serve one purpose, and they are unified in one unifying act of cognition. And that is called action. The parts exist for the whole, and therefore identified with it. . . . Oneness is attributed to the parts on the basis of the whole which is not real, because the parts, produced in sequence cannot co-

---

18 *VP* III.8.1.

19 *VP* III.8.4.

> exist. Therefore the verb "cooking" stand for collection of parts, like putting the vessel on fire, and so on, conceived by the mind as a unity. . . . The result is one and, therefore, parts lead to idea of action.

From the above explanations we note that there are some fundamental concepts involved in our understanding of the relation between time and action. First, the concept of action cannot be understood without reference to the notion of change that is in the form of sequence. So Helārāja commenting on the 30th *kārikā* of Kālasamuddeśa elucidates:

> As objects are constantly changing something is always produced and something else is always perishing . . . sequence is the primary property of actions but it is attributed to something else, viz. Time.

The world is characterized by action, but it should not be confused just with series of moments. Action in fact is One, a unification of moments, a sequence of moments – all having one purpose, i.e. action. It is One, for it has one purpose.[20] Therefore, just as a series of sequences do not make any change into an action, such sequence has to have one purpose or goal. As Bhartṛhari points out:

> A combination of various acts like eating appears to be interrupted or stopped by other actions coming in between. Though interrupted it is not finished because the ultimate result is not there. All actions appear to be mixed with other actions.[21]

Elucidating the idea Helārāja writes:

> Actions like eating consists of many parts arranged in a sequence and these acts seem to be interrupted by totally different actions such as laughing and talking. Up to

20 *VP* III.90.

21 *VP* III.82-83.

> satisfaction, the action of eating is one and though other actions may come in between, the action of eating is taken as a whole is considered uninterrupted.

Thus action is that which has one purpose. Moreover, the sequences of actions must have to be cognized as a whole at the mental level by the individual who cognizes it.

Again, the notions of past, present and future that help the cognition of events in an orderly manner are also understood in terms of action. Bhartṛhari says:

> Conditioned by action, Time attains the states of past, present and future.[22]

Time conditioned by action which after being initiated is over, is called the past. When conditioned by actions whose accessories are present, and which are expected to be initiated soon, is called future. When conditioned by actions, which have been initiated but not finished is called present. Even according to Bhartṛhari the constellations are due to the operation of time. So from the ontological angle Time and action are complementary concepts.

From the linguistic standpoint Time is equally the pivotal concept. For the human speech is sequential in nature. The language-in-use or *lokavyavahāra* needs to basic concepts – the speaker and the hearer. The speaker communicates his thought through speech. But the essential nature of the speech is that we utter words syllable by syllable in a sequence.[23] By the time we utter the second syllable the first syllable is lost. We cannot utter all the words to be communicated simultaneously. Similarly, the hearer listens to what the speaker has to say in a sequential way. Bhartṛhari, therefore, states clearly in his commentary on I.86:

---

22 *VP* III.9.37.

23 *VP* I.86.

> Nothing can be expressed through the word which has not assumed sequence.

Similarly with regard to Time he says:

> Whether it (word and the signified object) is only something having an existence in the mind or whether it has an existence outside the mind, expression in words is not possible without recourse to the notion of Time.[24]

This remark leads Helārāja to conclude that Bhartṛhari is not concerned with the philosophical notion of Time but only concerned with the grammatical factor which is the basis of tense distinction as "it was", "it is" and "it will". Our speech is not only sequential but also ordered in terms of the tense distinctions. The events are experienced as well as expressed in an orderly way with the help of the grammatical element of "tense". The use of tense, ultimately, refers to actions. We have noted earlier according to Bhartṛhari action is something which has parts arranged in a sequence. Such actions refer to processes which can only be denoted by verbs. The question is not whether actions actually have parts or not; but whether verbs present it as such or not. In our speech "the idea expressed by the verb is the main one because it is a process".[25] So we notice that in Bhartṛhari's analysis of the concept of Time the ontological and the linguistic dimensions run parallel. In his scheme of philosophy language reflects the reality. As I have already pointed out the world for Bhartṛhari is what the words present.

---

[24] *VP* III.9.58.

[25] *VP* III.9.99 (tr. Iyer).

Conclusion

In this book I have tried to offer a systematic account of the theory of *Kālaśakti* of Bhartṛhari keeping in the backdrop the alternative theories about the nature of *Kāla* as a concept. The use of the word *Kālaśakti* sometimes creates an impression that Bhartṛhari is interested in offering a mystical theory of *Kāla*, as one comes across in certain portions of *Mahābhārata* and Purāṇas. In popular perspective *Kāla* as a *śakti* (power) represents the invincible force that controls the human destiny. So it is often inferred that Bhartṛhari offers a theory of Kālavāda. Therefore I have made an effort to examine the concept of *Kālaśakti* of Bhartṛhari from all possible angles. Our discussion reveals that this concept is in no way associated with any form of mysticism or God-centric theory. It is purely a philosophical concept. It plays a crucial role in Bhartṛhari's philosophical analysis of language (semantics) as well as his metaphysics of linguistic non-dualism, viz. Śabdādvaitavāda. The notion of *Kālaśakti* serves as a major conceptual tool to untangle many complicated issues that are sometimes sidelined in some philosophical systems. For example, the concept of "change" continues to remain an enigma for both, the Realists as well as the Idealists. Similarly, the use of "time-words" in our linguistic usage points to the indispensability of the concept of time. This is evident from the fact that though many philosophical systems dismiss the conceptual independence of *Kāla* as a concept, they could not close their eyes to the problems raised by such "time-words" involving the use of the tense (past, present and future). Bhartṛhari's innovative analysis of the concept of *kāla* from the metaphysical as well as semantic angles brings to the foreground the deep nuances of the concept of *Kāla*.

Kālaśakti: The Semantic Facet

Bhartṛhari in his magnum opus – *Vākyapadīya* – treats the concept of *śabda* as the ultimate concern for his philosophical exploration. Being a self-acclaimed follower of the Vaiyākaraṇa tradition of the famous Pāṇini and Patañjali school of thought it might seem appropriate for him to elevate *śabda* to the level of the highest Reality, viz. *Śabdatattva-Brahman*. But none of his predecessors like Pāṇini, Patañjali or Kaiyaṭa aimed to transform the science of language to the level of a full-fledged philosophy of language. It seems that in ancient India a clear line of distinction was maintained between the Dārśanika and Vaiyākaraṇika traditions. There might have been certain levels of interaction between the two traditions as is obvious from the fact that Indian philosophers took a great interest in the phenomenon called language. *Śabda* (language) as a method of knowledge was a part of epistemology (whether it was offered an independent status or not is a separate issue). But *śabda-pramāṇa* acquired a new dimension in the philosophy of language of Bhartṛhari. It may be guessed that he might have derived his philosophical inspiration from Patañjali's *Mahābhāṣya*. He identifies himself as a *śabda-pramāṇaka*. But it appears that Patañjali has not used the word in the sense the philosophical tradition used the word *śabdapramāṇa*. The word has an epistemological tinge. But for Patañjali the word *śabdapramāṇaka* seems to have a different connotation as is obvious from his statement:

> *śabdapramāṇaka vayam yacchabda āha tad asmākam pramāṇam* ।
>
> We are the analysts of language. [Hence] what the words present is our only way of knowledge.

Commenting on Patañjali's statement, Bhartṛhari says:

> *kim asmākam vastugatena vicarena? arthastvasmākam yaḥ śabdenābhidhīyate* ।
>
> What is the use for us reflecting on the nature of things? The object for us is what the word presents.

This may be taken as the basic presupposition of his approach to philosophical analysis. But Bhartṛhari takes a giant leap forward to formulate a metaphysical superstructure on the concept of *śabda* in which the concept is elevated to the grand status of *Śabdatattva-Brahman*. Thereby he trespassed into the field of Darśana and provided a systematic form of non-dualistic metaphysics. Of course, the later Vaiyākaraṇikas like Somānanda and Utpalācārya criticized him for dabbling in metaphysics. But Bhartṛhari's motto of unfolding "what the word presents" is both insightful and philosophically illuminating. This led him to look at the phenomenal world including the experience and cognition of it in terms of word-potency. How we cognize the world is determined by the word-generated concepts. The concepts in turn could not be formed without the element of language. As a conclusion it follows that objects, their cognition and all our expressions and experiences of the phenomenal world are permeated by the One and unique linguistic principle (*Śabda-tattva Brahman*). But that is not the end of the story. Bhartṛhari was bold enough to deal with this concept of language at two separate yet interdependent levels – *śabda* as a *tattva* (metaphysical principle) as well as *śabda* as an act (*vyāpāra/vyavahāra*). As an act he perceived language as a communicative tool; as a living social affair. So he not only provided language-centric metaphysics but also a philosophy of language. He aimed to lay bare the structure of "how language functions". Matilal very rightly observes:

> The overall concern with how the language functions was not the chief concern of most Classical Indian philosophers, except for the Grammarians like Bhartṛhari.[1]

But he seems to present a partial account of Bhartṛhari's role. For, Bhartṛhari's concern goes beyond explicating how language functions. He aimed to provide a comprehensive account of the epistemology, metaphysics and semantics based on the conception of *Śabdatattva*. So his aim and objective are different from the other philosophers of language, past and present. In his analysis of language the demarcating line between metaphysics and what in modern terminology is called as the philosophy of language, is obliterated. This helps him to deal with the concept of *Kāla* at two parallel levels – the level of semantics and the level of metaphysics – with unusual ease.

The novelty of Bhartṛhari's philosophy of language consists in his attempt to present the entire analysis of "how language functions" in conformity with his metaphysical position. Though he virtually leaves no issue of the act of linguistic communication untouched, that is usually handled by the modern Western philosophers of language, viz. the relations between speaker and hearer, intention of the speaker and understanding by the hearer, word and meaning, word and world, language and thought, etc., all the relations converge at the unitary principle of the "Word-essence" (*Śabda-Brahman*). But he further brings to the focus another important feature of the act of linguistic communication, i.e. the sequential (*krama*) nature of the speech. To explicate how the speaker communicates his intention to the hearer the problem of sequentiality cannot be avoided. But this important issue has so far been avoided by the modern Western philosophers. Most probably the well-entrenched distinction between the

---

1 Matilal 1990: 4.

level of language and the level of thought; between the philosophy of language and the philosophy of mind, have forced them to shut themselves off from the issue of sequential nature of the speech-act. It might be assumed that in their opinion the problem associated with the sequential nature of speech properly belongs to the area of philosophy of mind or philosophical psychology. But the Indian philosophical tradition has never kept the two levels distinct. This helps Bhartṛhari to highlight on sequence (*krama*) in the level of language as an act, and bring in the concept of *kāla* to explain the nature of sequentiality (*krama*) in linguistic communication; and further to link sequentiality to non-sequentiality (*akrama*). Thus the concept *Kāla* serves as the principal tool for Bhartṛhari in his analysis of "how language functions".

As a linguistic non-dualist Bhartṛhari has to show that language is not just confined to the level of utterance or speech. The level of utterance (*vaikharī vāk*) is just the outer aspect of the linguistic expressibility. I have elaborated earlier that our speech is characterized by division between the meaning (*vācya*) and the word (*vācaka*). But language that human beings use for communication is not simply a string of spoken or written words. It is dead and sterile if not connected with the level of thought. Again, there has to be some link between what we say by words and what we mean; between the speaker's intention and hearer's understanding. The analysis of these issues is bound to point to a level deeper than the level of speech. This level is the level of thought. So the level of utterance (*vaikharī*) leads to a pre-verbal mental stage (*madhyamā*). It is a thought with same verbal contents, but unuttered. But *vaikharī* and *madhyamā* are not two distinct levels. There is interdependence between thought and language. Explaining Bhartṛhari's position regarding the relation between the level of speech and the level of thought B.K. Matilal very aptly remarks:

> Thought anchors language and language anchors thought. *Śabdanā*, languageing, is thinking; and thought "vibrates" through language.[2]

Both the levels are permeated by the element of language (*vāgrūpatā*). But the uttered speech with expressed discernible speech elements and the pre-verbal mental stage with the suppressed, though discernible speech elements, point to a stage where the distinction between *vācya* (meaning) and *vācaka* (word), between the level of pre-verbal thought and the verbal speech is obliterated. It is beyond *buddhi* (intellect). This stage is called *paśyantī*. This is the stage in which the potentiality for expressiveness is inherent. It is a non-differentiated principle. All the mental activities like cognition, experience, awareness, concept formation and finally consciousness are word-determined. Therefore the mental level finally points to a level of consciousness that refers to the principle of Word (*śabdatattva*) with the immense potentialities for diversification as well as sequentialization at each level. We have earlier discussed how according to Bhartṛhari even our very being, including awareness and thought, is determined by language. Whenever we express our thought through language it cannot be but in *krama*. Even our particular thoughts also occur sequentially. At the same time we note that the sense to be expressed is unitary in nature. Similarly, what is expressed sequentially is grasped by the hearer as a unitary "sense". So we pass from *krama* to non-*akrama* in the process of communications. This is evident from Bhartṛhari's remark:

> It (timeless Word-principle) has in fact the two powers of having or not having (attributes like sequence), the appearance of sequence in the non-sequential being merely dependent on pragmatic considerations – *Akrame kramanirvase vyavahāranibandhane*.[3]

---

2 Motilal 1990: 85.

3 *VP* II.32.

Kālaśakti: The Ontological Facet

From our discussion so far it follows that the concept of Time plays a crucial role in his philosophy of language so far as Bhartṛhari's notions of *krama* and *akrama* are concerned. Let us now have a re-look at the ontological dimension of Bhartṛhari's conception of Time as a *śakti*. For this we have to have a close look at the first three *kārikā*s of the first canto of his *Vākyapadīya*. In the introductory *kārikā* he introduces the idea of *Śabdatattva-Brahman* which though *One* evolves itself as process of the world. *Śabdatattva-Brahman* is asserted as the ground of the devolution of the world; and its transformation from the emergence (*sṛṣṭi*) to final re-absorption (*pralaya*). In next *kārikā* he introduces the notion of *śakti*. I have already discussed about the implications of the term *śakti* in Bhartṛhari's philosophy. So to put it in brief, *śakti* signifies the potentiality. Hence *śakti* has been described as non-different from *Śabdatattva-Brahman*. The third *kārikā* brings in the notion of *Kāla* as the primary power that is seen as the ground of the phenomenal world characterized by constant process of transformations like birth, destruction, etc. From the first three *kārikā*s we can gather the idea that Bhartṛhari conceives the metaphysical Reality to be of the nature of *Śabda-Brahman* that though One and unchanging is the ground of the process of the phenomenal world, characterized by diversity, differentiation and change.

Since Bhartṛhari conceives *Śabdatattva-Brahman* as the only substance/reality and *śakti* as the potentiality and power, it automatically follows that *śakti* is invested with the impulse that helps in transforming the potentiality of *Brahman*. This may help us to understand the logical link between *śakti* and *Śabdatattva-Brahman*. Through the concept of *śakti* Bhartṛhari intends to justify how the source of the multiplicity of the phenomenal world is inextricably related to the non-dual entity. In a sense *Śabdatattva-Brahman* may be seen as the womb of differentiated potentialities. The manifestation of the potentiality is not different even though in occurrence it may appear as separate. The effect is not separate from its original cause as the golden ornament is not different from the gold from which it is made. He enlists the powers of *Śabdatattva-Brahman* as *kāla* (time), *dik* (direction), *ākāśa* (space), *kriyā* (action), *abhyanujñā* (permission), *pratibandha* (suspension), *atīta* (past), *vartamāna* (present), *bhaviṣyata* (future), *samavāya* (inherence) and *sādhana* (instrument). Bhartṛhari introduces the notion of *śakti* with a view to explain the phenomenal world in which we move, live and have our being. All these powers can be divided into two categories – direct and indirect. Time, space, direction and action generally come under the direct powers; inherence, sequence, permission, suspension, past, present and future come under the indirect powers. However Bhartṛhari in consonance with his non-dualistic position always maintains that the *śakti* of the Reality Supreme can never be seen as different from its powers. For in the 4th *kārikā* he describes *Śabda-Brahman* as the "seed of all" (*sarvabīja*). This suggests that a multiplicity of powers of a substance does not affect the unity of substance. This becomes evident in the delineation of a substance (*dravya*). Bhartṛhari in the context of *dravya* says that even if a substance is connected with different actions its essence is not lost.[4] This view of Bhartṛhari on substance is based upon Patañjali's notion that when an essence (*tattva*) of certain thing is not lost even if different qualities manifest themselves in the thing, the thing is to be considered as substance. The essence (*ātmatattva*) of a substance is nothing but its self-identity, without which it would be neither what it is, nor be different from what it is not. A substance is that which possesses self-identity. It appears that the introduction of the notion of *śakti* is necessitated in order to obtain self-identity for a highest substance, i.e. *Śabda-Brahman*, to which

---

4 *VP* III.7.166.

it is attributed. Again, the notion of power is introduced in his metaphysics to account for the claim that the one substance can serve as the causal basis for producing multiple effects and to secure a self-identity for such a substance. Bhartṛhari goes one step further and considers *Brahman* as the *nimitta kāraṇa* of the phenomenal world (*prakriyā jagato yataḥ*) and also as the seed of all (*ekasya sarvabījasya*). But in case of phenomenal substance Bhartṛhari maintains a distinction between the substance and the cause, but in the metaphysical level he insists on non-distinction.

In the third *kārikā* he prioritizes *Kāla* as the first power of *śabdatattva* to enter into action in the process of transformation. *Kāla* as the first power is regarded as the initiator of six forms of transformations that is witnessed in the phenomenal world – birth, existence, change, growth, decay and destruction. Such transformations are possible through two primary functions of permission (*abhyanujñā*) and suspension (*pratibandha*) of *Kāla*. Without these two functions of the Time the world would have been a static world composed of a conglomeration of objects. So the picture of the world Bhartṛhari provides is not just a world of diversities but also of a process characterized by constant process of change. So he also emphasizes on two other functions (*vṛtti*) or power (*śakti*) of *Kāla*, viz. *krama* and *jarā* (decomposition). With these two *vṛtti*s he explains the world process in which objects and events constantly arise, sustain and ultimately come to an end. Despite attributing *svātantrya* (independence) to *Kālaśakti* in the final analysis he discards the independence of *Kāla* as it is transcendentally unreal. As long as we are talking of the phenomenal world with diversity and change, *Kāla* has reality.

We have already discussed how Bhartṛhari had both linguistic and ontological obligation to introduce the notion of *Kālaśakti* to explain the phenomenon called "change". He exhibits quite explicitly how at the level of ontology as well as semantics, there is a movement from *krama* to *akrama*. Though he conceives the phenomenal world as consisting of both the object (*mūrti-vivartta*) and states of the object (*kriyā-vivartta*), for him the objects are finally to be understood in terms of production, continuance and destruction. The states of the object determine the nature of an object. So world is not a conglomeration of diverse objects but diverse states of the objects. The world is a totality of facts or states of affairs (*kriyāvivartta*) rather than the objects. The states of affairs are conceptually connected with a process that implies change. Change on the other hand is conceptually dependent on time. So *Kālaśakti* is a pivotal concept in his metaphysics.

Bhartṛhari: The Dārśanika

The concept of Time as power can be said to be a unique contribution of Bhartṛhari to the philosophical tradition of India. It is a fact that most of the philosophical traditions – both realistic and idealistic – have brought in the notion of time to explicate their ontological stance regarding the nature of the reality as well as the phenomenal world. So some delineate it as substance, while others mark it out as atom; some present it as real while other conceive it just as a mental construct. But in no philosophical work the concept of time has been dealt with in such a detail as we notice in the case of Bhartṛhari's *Vākyapadīya* and specifically the section devoted to time, viz. Kālasamuddeśa. It is a fact, that the accredited schools of philosophy (*ṣaḍadarśana*) have never accepted Bhartṛhari as a Dārśanika but just as a Vaiyākaraṇika. Despite such discriminatory attitude historically, it is very difficult to deny the fact that he was one of the first systematic non-dualist (Advaitavādins) in Indian philosophical tradition. Our probe into his metaphysical perspective leaves no scope for doubt that he presents a well-etched non-dualistic system of thought. This is evident from the fact that philosophers like Jayanta

Bhaṭṭa, Śāntarakṣita, Vācaspati Miśra, Dīpaṅkara, Diṅnāga and Śaṅkara, who have been endorsed by the tradition as Dārśanikas, took up some of the metaphysical concepts of Bhartṛhari for scrutiny. Whether they do it for the purpose of refutation or for the purpose of support is immaterial. Dīpaṅkara of Vaibhāsika Buddhism quoted as well as examined Bhartṛhari's theory of *sphoṭa*. Similarly, Diṅnāga in his works *Traikālyaparīkṣā* and *Pramāṇa-Samuccaya* quotes profusely from Bhartṛhari's *Vākyapadīya*. Had Bhartṛhari's metaphysical concepts being philosophically inept they would not have been included within the fold of the philosophical deliberations of such eminent philosophers. In this context it is interesting to note his broad-minded approach to the method of doing philosophy. He humbly announces:

> *prajñāvivākam labhate bhinairāgāma darśanaiḥ* ।
> *kiyaddhā śākyamunnetuṁ svatarkamanudbhavata* ॥
> – II.483

> The intellect acquires critical acumen by familiarity with different traditions. How much does one really understand by merely following one's own reasoning only? – tr. Iyer

Here is a philosopher who does not dismiss every concept that is propounded by the other systems of thought just for the sake of exhibiting his dialectical skill. So even if he disagrees with the opponent's point of view he handles it with sympathy. This unusual humility on Bhartṛhari's part departs totally from the vigorous dialectical approach that was very common in the philosophical deliberations of Classical Indian philosophy. May be this modesty was misinterpreted as his weakness. It appears natural that his contributions in the area of metaphysics did not win the accolades from his philosophical brethren. So it continued to remain in a state of oblivion. If his philosophy of language is resurrected by the modern scholars of philosophy during the last few decades it is largely due to the fascination of the Western philosophers about the concept of language. But Bhartṛhari's metaphysical theories, especially his Śabdādvaitavāda, are no way less cogent than any other philosophical theory of the genre of the accredited philosophical systems of India. This is more evident in his theory of *Kāla*. An unbiased study of Bhartṛhari's philosophy of Time reveals that his theory works as a double-edged weapon that deals with the nature of the language and the nature of the reality in a parallel way. This was no mean task. Without a sharp philosophical and conceptual acumen such an an analysis would have turned into mystical rhapsody.

Bibliography

Texts (Original Works)

Abhidharmakoṣa and Bhāṣya by Vasubandhu I & II, ed. Swami Dwarikadasa Sastri, Varanasi: Bauddha Bharati, 1969.

Mahābhāṣya of Patañjali, ed. F. Keilhorn, Bombay, 1899.

Nyāyamanjarī of Jayantabhaṭṭa, Kashi Sanskrit Series, 1936.

Vaiśeṣikasūtra of Kaṇāda, ed. Muni Jambuvijayi, Gaekwad Oriental Series, 1961.

Vākyapadīya of Bhartṛhari, ed. K.V. Abhyankar and V.P. Limaye, Poona: University of Poona, 1965.

Vākyapadīya of Bhartṛhari, with commentary of Helārāja, kāṇḍa III, ed. K.A.S Iyer, Poona: Deccan College, 1966.

Vākyapadīya of Bhartṛhari, with commentary of Helārāja, kāṇḍa III, ed. K.A.S Iyer, Part II, Delhi: Motilal Banarsidass.

Vākyapadīya of Bhartṛhari with Vṛtti and Paddhati of Vṛṣabhadeva, kāṇḍa I, ed. K.A.S. Iyer, Poona: Deccan College, 1969.

Vākyapadīya, Kāṇḍa I with commentary *Bhāvapradīpa*, Pt. Suryanarayana Shukla.

Vākyapadīya, Pt. Suryanarayan Sukla, Benaras: Kashi Sanskrit Series, 1937.

Vākyapadīya, with commentary Ambākartṛ, Pt. Raghunatha Sharma, Part I, Benares, Sarasvati Bhavana Granthamala, 91, 1963.

Vākyapadīya, with commentary Ambākartṛ, Pt. Raghunatha Sharma, Part II, Benares, Sarasvati Bhavana Granthamala, 91, 1968-69.

Yoga-Sūtra of Patañjali with Vyāsa Bhāṣya, Poona: Ananda Asrama Sanskrit Series, 1932.

Secondary Literature

Aklujkar, A.N., 2001, "The Word Is the World: Nondualism in Indian Philosophy of Language", in *Philosophy East and West*, **51**.4: 452-73 (Hawaii).

Arapura, J.G., 1981, "Nāgārjuna and Bhartṛhari on Time", in *Hermeneutical Essays on Vedanta Topics*.

Balslev, Anindita, N., 2009, *A Study of Time in Indian Philosophy*, Delhi: Motilal Banarsidass.

Bhaduri, S., 1975, *Studies in Nyāya-Vaiśeṣika Metaphysics*, Poona: Bhandarkar Oriental Research Institute.

Bhartṛhari, 1967, *Mahabhāsya Dīpikā*, Part I, Poona: Bhandarkar Oriental Research Institute.

Bhate, S. and J. Bronkhorst, 1993, *Bhartṛhari: Philosopher and Grammarian*, Delhi: Motilal Banarsidass.

Bhattacharya, B.P., 1962, *A Study of Language and Meaning*, Calcutta: Progressive Publishers.

———, 1985, *Bhartṛhari's Vākyapadīya and Linguistic Monism*, Poona: Bhandarkar Research Institute.

Brahma-Sūtra Bhāṣya of Śrī Śaṅkarācārya, Swami Gambhirananda (tr.), Calcutta: Advaita Ashram, 1977.

Chakravarty, P.C., 1933a, *The Philosophy of Sanskrit Grammar*, Calcutta: University of Calcutta.

———, 1933b, *Linguistic Speculation of Hindus*, Calcutta: University of Calcutta.

Coomaraswamy, A. K., 1990, *Time and Eternity*, New Delhi: Indira Gandhi National Centre for the Arts.

———, 1992, "Time and Eternity in Hinduism and Buddhism", in *Time in Indian Philosophy*, ed. Hari Shankar Prasad, Delhi: Sri Satguru Prakasan.

Coward, H., 1982, "Time (*kāla*) in Bhartṛhari's Vākyapadīya", *Journal of Indian Philosophy*, **10**: 277-87.

Coward, H., 1990, *Sphoṭa Theory of Language*, Delhi: Motilal Banarsidass.

Coward, H. and K.K. Raja, 1990, *The Philosophy of Grammarians* (*Encyclopedia of Indian Philosophies*), vol. V, Delhi: Motilal Banarsidass.

Filliozat, P.S., 2009, "Time as Power of Word according to Bhartṛhari", in *Bhartrhari: Language, Thought and Reality*, ed. Mithilesh Caturvedi, Delhi: Motilal Banarsidass.

Herbert, G.S., 1978, *Time a Metaphysical Study*, Trivandrum: College Book House.

Herzberger, R., 1986, *Bhartṛhari and the Buddhists*, Dordrecht: Reidel.

Ivanov, Vladimir P., 2009, "Vidyā and Avidyā in Bhartṛhari's *Vākyapadīya*" in *Bhartṛhari: Language, Thought and Reality*, ed. Mithilesh Caturvedi, Delhi: Motilal Banarsidass.

Iyer, K.A.S., 1969, *Bhartṛhari: A Study of Vākyapadīya in the Light of Ancient Commentaries*, Poona: Deccan College.

———, 1965, *The Vākyapadīya of Bhartṛhari with Vṛtti*, Chapter I, Poona: Deccan College.

———, 1977, *Vākyapadīya of Bhartṛhari*, Kāṇḍa II, Delhi: Motilal Banarsidass.

———, 1971, *Vākyapadīya of Bhartṛhari*, Chapter III, pt. 1, Poona: Deccan College.

———, 1974, *Vākyapadīya of Bhartṛhari*, Chapter III, pt. II, Delhi: Motilal Banarsidass.

———, 1982, *The Vākyapadīya: Some Problems*, Poona: Deccan College.

Keith, A.B., 1992, "Time and Space in Nyāya-Vaiśeṣika" in *Time in Indian Philosophy*, ed. Hari Sankar Prasad.

Majumdar, P.K., 2007, *Bhartṛharir Darsane Kāler Dhāranā* (Bengali), Calcutta: Jadavpur University.

Matilal, B.K., 1990, *The Word and the World*, Delhi: Oxford University Press.

Monier-Williams, 1899, Moniter, *Sanskrit-English Dictionary*, Delhi: Motilal Banarsidass, 1993, reprint.

Mukhopadhyaya, P.K., 2009, "Does Time Have a Beginning: Some Inter Systematic General Observations", in Priyadarshi Patnaik et al. (ed.) *Time in Indian Culture: Diverse Perspective*, New Delhi: D.K. Printworld.

Ogaya, Hindeyo, 2009, "Bhartṛhari's Notion of Power", in *Bhartṛhari: Language, Thought and Reality*, ed. Mithilesh Caturvedi, Delhi: Motilal Banarsidass.

Panda, G.P., 1997, "The Concept of Time in Indian Grammatical Tradition (1)", *Sambhāsa*, **18**: 97-124.

———, 1999, "The Concept of Time in Indian Grammatical Tradition (2)", *Sambhāsa*, **20**.

———, 2003, "The Concept of Time in Indian Grammatical Tradition (3)", *Sambhāsa*, **23**.

Pandeya, R.C., 1963, *The Problem of Meaning in Indian Philosophy*, Delhi: Motilal Banarsidass.

Panikkar, Raimundo, 1976, "Time and History in the Tradition of India: Kāla and Krama" in *Culture and Time*, ed. L. Gaslet et al., Paris: UNESCO Press, 1976. Also reprinted in *Time in Indian Philosophy*, ed. Hari Shankar Prasad, Delhi: Sri Satguru Publications, 1992.

Patnaik, Priyadarshi et al. (eds.), 2009, *Time in Indian Culture: Diverse Perspectives*, New Delhi: D.K. Printworld.

Patnaik, Tandra, 1994, *Śabda: A Study of Bhartṛhari's Philosophy of Language*, Delhi: D.K. Printworld.

———, 1988, "Language, Thought and Communication: An Appraisal of Bhartṛhari's Theory of Language", *Indian Philosophical Quarterly*, **15**(3): 349-68.

———, 2009, "Time as Power: A Brief Survey of Bhartrhari's Metaphysics", in *Time in Indian Culture: Diverse Perspective*, New Delhi: D.K. Printworld.

———, 2009, "The Thought and Language: The Bhartṛharian Perpective", in *Bhartṛhari: Language , Thought and Reality*, ed. Mithilesh Caturvedi, Delhi: Motilal Banarsidass.

———, 1981, "The Idea of Power (Śakti) in the Vākyapadīya", *Bharatiya Vidya*, **41**: 75-79.

Pillai, K. Raghavan, 1971, *The Vākyapadīya: Critical Texts of Cantos I & II*, Delhi: Motilal Banarsidass.

Potter, Karl, 2008, *Encyclopedia of Indian Philosophies*, vol. IX: *Buddhist Philosophy from 350 to 600 A.D.*, Delhi: Motilal Banarsidass.

———, 1999, *Encyclopedia of Indian Philosophies*, vol. VIII: *Buddhist Philosophy from 100 to 350 A.D.*, Delhi: Motilal Banarsidass.

Potter, Karl, 1999, *Encyclopedia of Indian Philosophies*, vol.VIII, Delhi: Motilal Banarsidass.

Prasad, Hari Shankar, 1992, *Time in Indian Philosophy*, Delhi: Sri Satguru Publications.

———, 1991, *Essays on Time in Buddhism*, Delhi: Sri Satguru Publications.

Radhakrishnan, S., 1977, *The Bhagavadgita*, Bombay: Blackie and Sons (India) Ltd.

Raja, K. Kunjunni, 1963, *Indian Theories of Meaning*, Adyar: Adyar Library.

———, 1997, "Bhatrhari's Philosophy of Language: Sphoṭavada and Śabdabrahmavāda: Are They Related", in *India and Beyond: Essays in Honour of Frits Staal*, London: Kegan Paul.

Raju, P.T., 1985, *Structural Depths of Indian Thought*, New Delhi: South Asian Publishers.

Ramasawmi Sastry, V.A., 1938, "Bhartṛhari: A Pre-Śankarian Advaitin", *Annamalai University Journal*, VIII.

Sastri, Gaurinatha, 1959, *The Philosophy of Word and Meaning*, Calcutta: Calcutta Sanskrit College.

———, 1959, "The Doctrine of Śabda Brahma: A Criticism by Jayanta Bhaṭṭa", in *Indian Historical Quarterly*, XV.

Sastri, Satyabrata, 1958, "The Conception of Time according to Bhartrhari", *Annals of the Bhandarkar Oriental Research Institute*.

Schayer, Stanislaw, 1991, "Contributions to the Problem of Time in Indian Philosophy", in *Essays on Time in Buddhism*, ed. H.S. Prasad, Delhi: Sri Satguru Publications.

Sen, Sanat Kumar, 1968, "Time in Sāṁkhya-Yoga", *International Philosophical Quarterly*; reprinted in *Time in Indian Philosophy*, ed. Prasad, 1992.

Sharma, Peri Sarveswara, 1972, *Kālasamuddeśa of Bhartṛhari's Vākyapadīya*, Delhi: Motilal Banarasidass.

Sharma, Virendra, 1977, *Vākyapadīya: Sambhandha Samuddeśa*, Punjab University Indological Series.

Shukla, B.S., 1956, "The Concept of Time according to Bhartṛhari", *Proceedings of All India Oriental Conference*, **17**: 379-84.

Stcherbatsky, F.Th., 2008, *Buddhist Logic*, Delhi: Low Price Publications.

Strawson, P.F., 1992, *Analysis and Metaphysics*, Oxford: Oxford University Press.

Index